FIGHTER PILOT

Alex Vraciu

FIGHTER PILOT

THE WORLD WAR II CAREER OF
ALEX VRACIU

RAY E. BOOMHOWER

INDIANA HISTORICAL SOCIETY PRESS · INDIANAPOLIS 2010

Printed in the United States of America

This book is a publication of the
Indiana Historical Society Press
Eugene and Marilyn Glick Indiana History Center
450 West Ohio Street
Indianapolis, Indiana 46202-3269 USA
www.indianahistory.org
Telephone orders 1-800-447-1830
Fax orders 1-317-234-0562
Online orders @ http://shop.indianahistory.org

The paper in this publication meets the minimum requirements of American National
Standard for Information Sciences—Permanence of Paper for Printed Library Materials,
ANSI Z39. 48 – 1984

Library of Congress Cataloging-in-Publication Data

Boomhower, Ray E., 1959–
Fighter pilot : the World War II career of Alex Vraciu / Ray E. Boomhower.
        p. cm.
Includes bibliographical references and index.
ISBN 978-0-87195-282-0 (cloth : alk. paper)
1. Vraciu, Alexander. 2. United States. Navy. Fighting Squadron 6.
3. World War, 1939-1945—Aerial operations, American. 4. World War,
1939-1945—Naval operations, American. 5. World War,
1939-1945—Campaigns—Pacific Area. 6. Air pilots, Military—United
States—Biography. 7. United States. Navy—Biography. 8.
Indiana—Biography. I. Title.
D790.3756th .B66 2010
940.54'5973092—dc22
[B]
                                                2009035217

For Doug Clanin in recognition of his
longtime service to collecting and preserving
the memories of World War II veterans.

A Navy Flyer's Creed

I am a United States Navy flyer.

My countrymen built the best airplane in the world and entrusted it to me. They trained me to fly it. I will use it to the absolute limit of my power.

With my fellow pilots, air crews, and deck crews, my plane and I will do anything necessary to carry out our tremendous responsibilities. I will always remember we are part of an unbeatable combat team—the United States Navy.

When the going is fast and tough, I will not falter. I will be uncompromising in every blow I strike. I will be humble in victory. I am a United States Navy flyer. I have dedicated myself to my country, with its many millions of all races, colors, and creeds. They and their way of life are worthy of my greatest protective effort.

I ask the help of God in making that effort great enough.

Published with the support of the East Chicago Washington High School Alumni Association, Foundations of East Chicago, and Community Foundation of Northwest Indiana.

Contents

1

"AIR RAID! NO DRILL!"

Early in the morning of Sunday, December 7, 1941, nine-year-old Joan Zuber, the daughter of a U.S. Marine officer stationed at Pearl Harbor, the major American naval base in the Hawaiian Islands, started her day by opening the pages of a favorite book. She had just settled back to begin her reading when, out of the corner of her eye, she saw a "grayish-black column of smoke. Something was burning."

Zuber dropped her book and ran outside to see what was happening. Looking over the bushes in her yard toward Luke Field, the navy's airbase on Ford Island located in the center of the harbor, she could see smoke and flames rising into the sky, filling it with a large, black cloud. Although her first thought was to run back inside the house to tell her mother what was happening, she instead remained outside. "Just then a strange plane with red balls on the sides of its body swooped low over my head, diving toward the masts of the [battleships] *West Virginia* and *Tennessee*," Zuber remembered. "What plane was that? What was it doing flying so low?"

The plane Zuber saw streaking toward the American ships was part of a force unleashed in two waves from six aircraft carriers from the Empire of Japan. The surprise attack—undertaken without a formal declaration of war—by the enemy aircraft aimed to quickly swoop down and destroy the 130 vessels of the United States' Pacific Fleet—ships that Japanese Fleet Admiral Isoroku Yamamoto, in charge of planning the strike, called "a dagger pointed at our [Japan's] throat."

That "dagger" Yamamoto had been so worried about suffered horribly from the enemy onslaught on December 7. An armor-piercing bomb slammed into the battleship USS *Arizona*. The bomb sliced through the ship and ignited its forward ammunition magazine, setting off a huge explosion, killing 1,177 crew members. Although unprepared for the onslaught, American forces shot down twenty-nine Japanese aircraft. They suffered, however, the loss of two battleships (the *Arizona* and *Oklahoma*) and severe damage to another six battleships, as well as having approximately two hundred airplanes destroyed on the ground and approximately 3,500 servicemen either killed or wounded. "We may conclude," a Japanese officer said of the attack, "that the results we anticipated have been achieved."

News of the disaster at Pearl Harbor made its way slowly from Hawaii (then a U.S. territory) to the continental United States. At 2:26 p.m., Len Sterling, staff announcer for WOR Radio in New York, interrupted a broadcast of a professional football game between the Brooklyn Dodgers and New York Giants at the Polo Grounds to read the following bulletin from the United Press news agency: "The Japanese have attacked Pearl Harbor, Hawaii, by air, President [Franklin D.] Roosevelt has just announced."

Soon, other radio stations broadcast the momentous news to a stunned and disbelieving nation. Some even thought that broadcasters were trying to pull a hoax similar to the one Orson Welles had done with his famous October 30, 1938, *War of the Worlds* broadcast on Halloween that tricked some Americans into thinking the nation was being invaded by Martians. Others, however, were determined to avenge the defeat and began lining up at recruiting centers for the army, navy, and marines.

Clockwise from top: Disregarding bombs from Japanese planes, American sailors at Pearl Harbor try to extinguish a fire on the USS *West Virginia*; the battleship USS *Arizona* sinks to the bottom of the harbor; and a view of U.S. Navy vessels under attack.

After meeting with members of his administration and congressional leaders at the White House to discuss the attack, Roosevelt began dictating the speech he would make to Congress on December 8 asking legislators for a declaration of war against Japan (the measure passed with only one dissenting vote, from Congresswoman Jeannette Rankin of Montana). The message began: "Yesterday, December 7, 1941—a date which will live in infamy—the United States of America was suddenly and deliberately attacked by naval and air forces of the Empire of Japan. The United States was at peace with that nation and, at the solicitation of Japan, was still in conversation with its Government and its Emperor looking toward the maintenance of peace in the Pacific." Three days later, Germany and Italy declared war on the United States. America had entered World War II.

Late in the evening of December 7, Roosevelt met after dinner with Edward R. Murrow, the newsman made famous by his dramatic live reports from London, England, as it was being bombed by the Germans. The president told Murrow of the tremendous losses at Pearl Harbor and expressed his disbelief that the Japanese could achieve such a total surprise with its strike on a major American military base. "Our planes were destroyed *on the ground*!" Roosevelt exclaimed. "On the *ground*!"

In December 1941 twenty-three-year-old Alex Vraciu (rhymes with cashew), born in East Chicago, Indiana, in the part called Indiana Harbor, the second child and only son of a longtime police officer in that community, was temporarily stationed at the Glenview Naval Air Station in Illinois. There he was undergoing preliminary training to become a fully qualified navy pilot. Vraciu had recently graduated from DePauw University in Greencastle, Indiana, where he was respected for his athletic ability, but best known for having a wicked sense of humor and for playing an elaborate prank with his fraternity brothers on a psychology professor that received nationwide attention.

During a summer break from his college studies between his junior and senior year at DePauw, Vraciu had earned a private pilot's license through the federal government's Civilian Pilot Training program—training that came in handy with America's entry into the war. Relaxing at the home of his uncle in the Chicago suburbs that Sunday in December, Vraciu remembered being as shocked as millions of other Americans were when they heard the news over the radio about the disaster at Pearl Harbor. "I had a big mad on . . . after Pearl Harbor,"

Above: President Franklin D. Roosevelt signs the declaration of war against the Empire of Japan. Right: A formal portrait of Alex Vraciu in the uniform of a World War II naval officer.

recalled Vraciu, whose anger also grew as he later saw his friends fall to Japanese gunfire. He vowed to gain a measure of revenge on the enemy, and his proud uncle promised to pay him $100 for each Japanese aircraft he destroyed.

The Japanese attack on Pearl Harbor appeared to be a great success. It had, however, some fatal flaws. Enemy planes had failed to destroy the vital fuel, ammunition, and repair facilities at the base. In addition, what were to become the most important ships in the American Pacific Fleet—aircraft carriers—were not there. The carriers *Enterprise*, *Lexington*, and *Saratoga* were away from Pearl Harbor and had survived intact. In the long struggle to defeat Japan, the aircraft carrier, with its complement of fighters, dive bombers, and torpedo planes, soon replaced the battleship as the most important tool in the American navy's arsenal.

Over the next few years, U.S. carriers were able to take the war directly to the enemy, first, in air attacks on far-flung Japanese bases, and later in protecting troops from the U.S. Marine Corps and Army as they stormed ashore to wrest heavily defended Pacific islands and atolls from their determined defenders. And, for the first time in naval history, surface forces engaged in battle without seeing one another. Instead, the aircraft launched from carriers led the attack, dropping bombs and torpedoes and strafing enemy ships with machine-gun fire.

Vraciu earned his navy wings in August 1942 and eventually became one of the more than three hundred navy pilots flying from U.S. carriers in the Pacific Theater to earn the title of ace (downing five confirmed enemy aircraft in aerial combat). He did so while flying the famous F6F Hellcat fighter plane built by the Grumman Aircraft Company of Bethpage, New York. In the early days of the war, the dreaded Japanese Mitsubishi Zero, a lightweight and nimble enemy

A navy pilot in his Grumman F6F Hellcat fighter plane waits for the signal to launch from a U.S. aircraft carrier somewhere in the Pacific Ocean. The Hellcat proved to be so dependable that it remained in navy service until the early 1950s.

airplane, had outclassed U.S. pilots flying such fighter aircraft in the Pacific as the Brewster F2A Buffalo, the Grumman F4F Wildcat, and the Curtiss P-40 Warhawk.

Designed to take on and defeat the Zero, the Hellcat, under the control of pilots such as Vraciu, turned the tide for the Americans in the war against the Japanese. "The Hellcat gave us not only the speed, range, and climb to compete successfully against the Zero," Vraciu noted, "but it could dictate the rules of combat." One Hellcat pilot compared flying the plane to being as easy and comfortable as "sitting in your mother's lap," while another spoke for many navy pilots when he exclaimed: "I love this airplane so much that if it could cook I'd marry it." By the war's end, for every Hellcat downed by the Japanese, the blue-painted Grumman fighter shot down nineteen of the enemy, the greatest kill ratio of any airplane in any war in any country. "All in all, the Hellcat was a perfect carrier plane, and we loved it!" said Vraciu.

While stationed in Hawaii early on during his service, Vraciu became the wingman of a famous pilot, Lieutenant Commander Edward "Butch" O'Hare, who had been awarded his country's highest honor, the Congressional Medal of Honor, for shooting down five Japanese bombers. "We were training with a legend. I learned my trade from one of the *best*!" Vraciu said of O'Hare, for whom O'Hare International Airport in Chicago is named. "He taught you lessons you didn't realize until you are fighting in combat yourself that may have saved your life."

Vraciu learned well with O'Hare's Fighting Squadron 3 (later changed to 6). Finally making it into combat at the end of August 1943 as part of a strafing raid on a Japanese base on Marcus Island, Vraciu earned his first aerial victory by shooting down a Zero in October during a mission against Wake Island. Shortly thereafter, O'Hare received a promotion to Air Group Commander serving aboard another carrier. Vraciu's feud with his opponents in the air had become much more personal when he learned that his mentor, O'Hare, had been killed while pioneering night fighting off carriers on November 26, 1943, apparently by a Japanese G4M Mitsubishi Betty bomber during a confused night battle. He vowed to shoot down ten of the same aircraft to avenge O'Hare's death.

The Hoosier pilot began to make good on his promise and achieved ace status on January 29, 1944, when he downed three Betty bombers near Kwajalein. "Between the vow on Butch and Pearl Harbor, I think that probably was the biggest single motivator—driving force— in my life as to why I preferred to be out there rather than back home," Vraciu later explained. "I'd rather be in combat. That's really what it did to me. That's the honest truth."

Possessed with keen eyesight, quick reflexes, excellent shooting instincts, and a knack for finding his opponent's weak spot, Vraciu became skilled in the deadly game of destroying the enemy in the skies over the Pacific Ocean. "That was our job," he noted. "That is what we were trained to do. You can't be squeamish about the thing or you don't belong in a cockpit of that kind of an airplane [a fighter]. Nobody told you it was going to be an easy job."

For a period of four months in 1944, Vraciu stood as the leading ace in the U.S. Navy. He shot down nineteen enemy airplanes in the air, destroyed an additional twenty-one on the ground, and sank a large Japanese merchant ship with a well-placed bomb hit. He also earned a distinction as "Grumman's Best Customer," as he twice had to ditch his Hellcat in the ocean due to battle damage or mechanical failure, and two of the carriers he served on were torpedoed (but not sunk) by the Japanese.

Perhaps Vraciu's most notable achievement in the war came on the morning of June 19, 1944, while part of a carrier task force protecting American forces landing on Saipan in the Mariana Islands. Facing an attack from a large Japanese fleet, Vraciu and other American pilots rushed to their planes to protect the American ships in a lopsided air battle that became known as the Great Marianas Turkey Shoot.

Calling the mission a "once-in-a-lifetime fighter pilot's dream" when he spotted a large mass of enemy planes bearing down on the U.S. fleet, Vraciu, launched from the USS *Lexington*, pounced on

An official navy photograph captures Vraciu climbing out of the cockpit of his F6F-3 Hellcat aboard the USS *Lexington* in late July 1944. The plane displays nineteen Japanese flags, indicating the number of enemy aircraft Vraciu had shot down.

the Japanese and shot down six Japanese dive-bombers in just eight minutes. "I looked ahead," Vraciu told a *Chicago Tribune* reporter. "There was nothing but Hellcats in the sky. I looked back. Up above were curving vapor trails. And down on the sea, in a pattern 35 miles long, was a series of flaming dots where oil slicks were burning."

Vraciu had accomplished this stunning feat despite a number of mechanical difficulties. Engine trouble caused his windshield to be smeared with oil, which meant he had to fly his Hellcat close to the enemy so he could see what he was aiming at. Later he also learned that he flew his mission with his plane's wings not securely locked into place (aircraft serving on carriers usually had folding wings in order to be stored in the tight confines of the ship). Returning to the *Lexington*, Vraciu found that he had used just 360 rounds of ammunition from his Hellcat's six .50-caliber machine guns—a display of shooting Pacific War historian Barrett Tillman labeled as "world-class marksmanship."

His exploits in the air made Vraciu a hero back home and earned him the Navy Cross, the second highest award given for extraordinary courage in battle against the enemy. Chicago newspapers were quick to inform their readers about his victories and claim him as one of their own. City officials in East Chicago, not wanting to have their favorite son claimed by the big city to the west, made sure to honor Vraciu with a welcome-home celebration that saw approximately six thousand people jam Block Stadium and featured appearances by local, state, and national politicians. "I'd rather do without that welcome," a reluctant Vraciu told East Chicago mayor Frank Migas. "I'd rather just saunter down the street."

The hometown celebration did have a bright spot for Vraciu, however. As the parade in his honor passed a home on East 142nd Street in Indiana Harbor, the navy pilot jumped out of the car and ran up to greet the young daughter of a neighbor he knew, Margaret Horn, who instead pointed to her elder sister, Kathryn. This chance meeting resulted in a whirlwind courtship, and Vraciu married Kathryn Horn on August 24, 1944.

Vraciu could not stay out of action for long. "I worked too hard to get out there," he remembered, "and if one is eager, it doesn't seem unnatural to want to remain in the forward area. All good fighter pilots naturally want to be where the action is." His luck, however, finally ran

COURTESY ALEX VRACIU

Vraciu is joined by his family on his return home after becoming the navy's leading ace. Joining Vraciu (center) are, from left to right: Mr. and Mrs. John Tincu, Vraciu's aunt and uncle; Vraciu's mother, Maria; Vraciu's father, Alexander; his sister, Betty; and Betty's husband, Thomas Gall.

out on December 14, 1944, during a strafing run against a Japanese airfield before the American invasion to retake the Philippines. Heavy antiaircraft fire hit his Hellcat, puncturing his oil tank. "I knew I had it," he remembered. "Oil was gushing out and going all over my canopy, and my oil pressure was rapidly dropping. There was no way I'd be able to get back to my carrier."

After safely bailing out of his stricken plane, Vraciu parachuted to the ground close to enemy-held territory near Mount Pinatubo, an

COURTESY ALEX VRACIU

A bearded Vraciu shows off a Japanese two-handed sword to fellow navy pilots Lieutenant W. C. Kelly (left) and Ensign F. L. Muro (center). Vraciu acquired the sword from a guerrilla fighter after being shot down on the island of Luzon in the Philippines.

active volcano. Luckily he was almost immediately rushed to safety by a small group of U.S. Army in the Far East guerrillas, who had been battling the Japanese in the area for the past few years. The small force was under the command of an American who had escaped from Japanese capture after the surrender of U.S. troops in 1942.

The navy flyer spent the next five weeks with the guerrillas, receiving the honorary rank of brevet major while with them. "For the final week of this episode," Vraciu recalled, "I found myself in command of 180 men, dodging Japanese to meet General [Douglas] MacArthur's advancing Americans." He finally marched into an American camp carrying with him a captured Japanese Luger pistol and sword. Unfortunately, because of his time behind enemy lines, Vraciu was prevented by navy officials from participating in the last missions against the Japanese home islands. When the war finally ended with Japan's surrender on August 14, 1945, Vraciu, the navy's fourth-ranking ace, was in the United States flying as a test pilot at the Naval Air Test Center in Patuxent River, Maryland.

After the war, Vraciu remained in the navy, working in the Pentagon in Washington, D.C. During the 1950s he reached the "ultimate desire of all fighter pilots" when he took command of his own squadron, becoming the leader of Fighter Squadron 51, flying North American FJ-3 Fury jet fighters. Retiring from the navy in 1964 with the rank of commander, Vraciu began a career in banking for Wells Fargo in California. Today, at the age of ninety-one, he lives in Danville, California, in the home where he and his late wife retired after raising five children (three daughters and two sons). He enjoys spending time with his eleven grandchildren and six great-grandchildren.

Vraciu during his time as commander of Fighter Squadron 51, July 1957, San Diego, California. "I had the best fighter squadron," Vraciu said of his command.

Vraciu keeps the memory of his service as part of the World War II generation alive through speaking appearances before various organizations and school groups. His experiences as a fighter pilot in the Pacific continue to be a large part of his life, as his autograph is sought after by fans from around the world. Sometimes, Vraciu even finds himself practicing his old runs on enemy aircraft on the car ahead of him on the off ramp of freeways. The tragedy of Pearl Harbor also haunts him, and he remains troubled by Japan's continuing refusal to apologize for the attack.

2

THE REGION

In 1895 a group of Chicago investors organized the Lake Michigan Land Company and began buying property along the southern shore of Lake Michigan in northwestern Indiana near the Twin City, as the communities of East Chicago and Indiana Harbor in Lake County were then known. Within a few years, the company had bought approximately 1,300 acres and, in 1901, it made arrangements with Inland Steel to build a new steel mill in Indiana Harbor.

Construction crews soon turned the often swampy and sandy area into land suitable for a steel mill. By 1904 more than a thousand workers were employed at Inland Steel's operation. Other heavy industry followed, including the building of a huge steel plant by the U.S. Steel Corporation in the new city of Gary, named after Judge Elbert H. Gary, chairman of the corporation's board of directors. Lake County, much of which is known as the Calumet Region, had become one of Indiana's leading industrial centers, growing from a population of 12,800 in 1905 to 87,000 by 1916.

The jobs created by the steel and other industries attracted the attention of a new kind of immigrant seeking a better life in the United States. Between 1880 and 1920, immigrants from such southern and eastern European countries as Italy, Greece, Russia, Bulgaria, Austria, Hungary, and Romania flocked to America. They competed for jobs working long hours for low pay, but offered greater opportunity than what had been available in their former countries. As one historian noted, a peasant worker from a village in a country such as Romania "realized he could make as much in one day in America as he did for ten days of work in the fields at home."

Many immigrants first landed in America at Ellis Island on the East Coast and worked their way across the country at a variety of jobs before settling down. One of these was Alexander Vraciu Sr. from the village of Poiana near the Transylvanian Mountains in Romania. After settling near Chicago, Vraciu met and married Maria Tincu, a young Romanian woman. The couple moved to Indiana Harbor, where their second child, a boy named Alexander, like his father, was born on November 2, 1918, just nine days before the end of World War I (a daughter, Betty, had been born almost a year and a half earlier).

Above: A train pulls into the Lake Shore railroad station at Indiana Harbor, Indiana. The Inland Steel Company is located behind the station. Right: Workers gather at the entrance to the Inland Steel Company.

Early photographs of Vraciu including (clockwise from left to right) a family portrait with his mother, father, and sister; a young Vraciu posing with a puppy; and Vraciu and his sister flanking their mother.

The senior Vraciu prospered in his new country. He was able to buy several properties in the area, including a three-story hotel, and eventually moved his family from their old Pennsylvania Avenue neighborhood on the wrong side of the railroad tracks to a home in Indiana Harbor's prestigious Park Addition district. When he was seven or eight years old, young Alex went with his family for an extended visit to Romania, where he attended school and learned the local language. For Alex, however, his home in Indiana Harbor offered everything a young boy could want. "It was the most cosmopolitan area probably in the whole country—every nationality in the whole world," he remembered. "We used to call each other names, but nobody got angry. They'd just turn around and give you a bad one [name], too."

Like many young boys who grew up in the years after World War I, Vraciu thrilled to the stories of the great pilots that had battled in the skies over France. These included such American heroes as Eddie Rickenbacker, the former race-car driver who had shot down twenty-six German planes with the Ninety-fourth Aero Squadron, becoming

Purdue University president Edward C. Elliott and famed aviator Amelia Earhart hold a model of the flying laboratory built for Earhart with the aid of the Purdue Research Foundation. Elliott brought Earhart to Purdue in the 1930s to work as a counselor for the university's female students.

America's "Ace of Aces." The pilots who fought overseas returned home to take jobs flying new airmail routes or barnstormed across the country thrilling crowds with such risky aerial stunts as wing walking and flying upside down, often in surplus Curtiss JN-4 Jenny biplanes from the war.

Americans also were enthralled by the exploits of Charles Lindbergh, whose historic May 20, 1927, nonstop solo flight across the Atlantic Ocean onboard the *Spirit of Saint Louis* drew worldwide attention. Other pilots, famous names such as Amelia Earhart, Wiley Post, Richard Bird, and Howard Hughes, followed in Lindbergh's wake, attempting to break records in this new venture. It was during this golden age of aviation that Vraciu remembers his father paying $2 for him to take his first flight in an old biplane.

The collapse of the stock market on October 29, 1929, an event known as Black Tuesday, began a long economic decline for the United States and the rest of the world. Prices for farm goods fell and millions of Americans found themselves out of work. The years known as the Great Depression were particularly tough on the Calumet Region. The steel industry, the lifeblood of the area, was operating at only 15 percent of its capacity by 1932. A number of banks in Lake County failed, and cities could not afford to pay the salaries of municipal employees such as schoolteachers.

Those who lived in the Calumet Region during the depression remember a time of suffering and hunger for many. Families were evicted from their homes when they could no longer pay their rent, and fathers sometimes abandoned their wives and children because the shame of being unable to provide for them proved to be too much to endure. Housewives used coffee grounds over and over until cups of coffee tasted like plain water, and youngsters scavenged in garbage cans for discarded orange peels to eat. An East Chicago native who grew up during this time recalled one day when his father returned home with a bag of flour. He and his brothers were so hungry that they "ripped open the bag and ate it just like that."

The tough times affected the Vraciu family. Alex's father had to sell a number of the properties he owned, and the family moved back to their old Pennsylvania Avenue neighborhood. "Somehow, we always existed," said Vraciu, "and it wasn't to the point that you were in grave jeopardy. I guess back in those days, you never really worried about those things, you took it as it came along." Fortunately, his father was able to find a job with the East Chicago police force and the family always managed to have food on the table.

As a student at Washington High School in East Chicago, Vraciu excelled both in the classroom and on the athletic field. Russell F.

Children line up at an East Chicago south-side soup kitchen during the height of the Great Depression. Soup kitchens were a familiar sight in America during the late 1920s and early 1930s, as communities struggled to feed often starving citizens. Mobster Al Capone sponsored a soup kitchen in Chicago to help with his image.

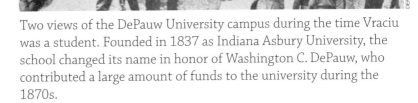

Two views of the DePauw University campus during the time Vraciu was a student. Founded in 1837 as Indiana Asbury University, the school changed its name in honor of Washington C. DePauw, who contributed a large amount of funds to the university during the 1870s.

Robinson, principal at the school, described Alex as "always a neat appearing lad, high strung, high spirited," as well as possessing "a very quick reaction time, both mental and physical." President of the National Honor Society, Vraciu also served as editor in chief of the school's yearbook, *The Anvil*, as a senior in 1937. He ran the quarter-mile, low hurdles, and mile relay as a member of the track team and also played an important role on a tennis squad that was undefeated and won the Western Division of Northern Indiana under coaches John Moore and Herman Dickes. In a playoff for the championship with Mishawaka High School, however, Vraciu and his team lost by a score of four matches to one.

Vraciu did well enough academically in high school to earn a four-year Rector Scholarship to DePauw University, a private college founded in 1837 by the Methodist Church and located in Greencastle, Indiana. In 1919 Edward Rector, a member of the university's board of trustees, donated money to provide scholarships to DePauw each year for a hundred of the brightest male graduates of Indiana high schools. Vraciu said that if he had not been fortunate enough to win the scholarship, he probably would have ended up going to either Purdue University in West Lafayette or Indiana University in Bloomington.

Even with a scholarship Vraciu, a premed major to start with, worked a variety of jobs at DePauw to make ends meet. He served as the headwaiter at the Delta Chi fraternity for room and board for three years and ran a mimeograph machine making copies for officials and professors in the college's administration building. To save money, he sent his laundry home for his mother to do.

As he had in high school, Vraciu ran on the track team while at DePauw. He also tried a sport that his mother and father had forbid him to play—football. "I was even on the basketball team for a while, because I never really had a crack at that back in high school," Vraciu said. "My grades were starting to slip in the middle of the year, so I had to drop that and make sure that I maintained my scholarship." He remained on the football team, however, playing linebacker on defense and halfback on offense during his freshman and sophomore years. "We played it both ways in those days," Vraciu noted.

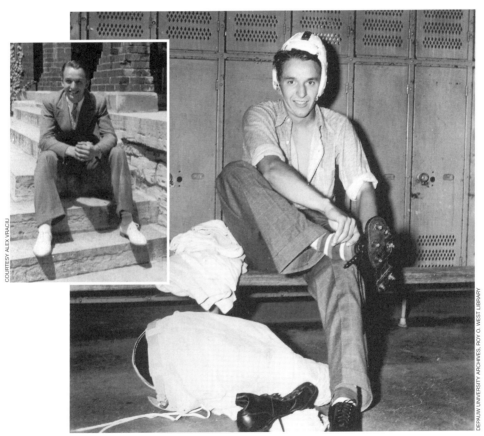

Above: Vraciu puts on his football cleats in this publicity photograph from DePauw in 1938. In those days, football players wore helmets without facemasks. **Inset:** Vraciu sits on the steps of Villa Lante, the Italian-style fraternity house of Delta Chi at DePauw.

A photographer captures Vraciu leaping from the second-story window of Asbury Hall at DePauw during a prank he played on his psychology teacher, Paul J. Fay. Vraciu's Delta Chi fraternity brothers held a tarpaulin on which he landed, safe and sound.

During the freshman game against Wabash College, Vraciu surprised one of his best friends from Washington High School, Bill Sabo, who did not know he played football for DePauw. "When I came out in uniform against him, I didn't say anything until I tackled him the first time," said Vraciu. "I thought he'd die when he saw who I was. We talked about that a few times over the years."

Football is a rough sport and in the sophomore game against Anderson College Vraciu injured his right knee. He had the knee operated on twice during the next two Christmas vacation periods and spent seven weeks in a cast each time, hobbling around the campus on crutches. By participating in track, Vraciu was able to build his knee up to good shape again. Throughout the healing process, he never told his parents about what had happened.

Vraciu's mischievous sense of humor also displayed itself during the spring of his sophomore year in a psychology class he took with Professor Paul J. Fay. Throughout the class Fay had attempted to show his students what poor observers they were by springing surprises on them and then making them describe what had happened. Vraciu was challenged by these tests and one day, while walking back to the Delta Chi house on South Locust Street with a few of his fraternity brothers who were also in the class, he asked them: "Why don't we pull one on him [Fay]?" His friends told him he was crazy, but Vraciu plotted his revenge, obtaining a tarpaulin from the Greencastle railway express office and telling the university's public relations office in confidence what he planned on doing.

The psychology class met on the second floor of Asbury Hall. Students were seated in reverse alphabetical order, so Vraciu sat near the front of the classroom. Fay was talking near the blackboard when Vraciu began his stunt. He carefully took off his watch and placed it on one of the seats in front of him. ("I didn't care about my neck," Vraciu laughed. "I was worried about my wristwatch. Isn't that silly?") He lifted up the back part of the chair in front of him, and brought it down to make a sharp noise. With a wild look in his eye, Vraciu then announced to the class in a strong voice: "I can't take this any longer!"

The prankster must have been convincing, because many of the students in the class were urging him to stop as he began to climb into an open window in the front of the room near the blackboard. Vraciu took a look down to make sure that his fraternity brothers were below holding the tarpaulin ("I'm not stupid," Vraciu said) and picked up an eraser from the blackboard to toss at anyone who might try and stop

U.S. NATIONAL ARCHIVES

German leader Adolf Hitler is joined by his fellow fascist dictator Benito Mussolini from Italy during a visit Mussolini made to Munich, Germany, in June 1940. Germany, Italy, and Japan were allies during World War II, known as the Axis Powers.

him. When the surprised Professor Fay started walking toward him, Vraciu jumped from the window, causing one of the girls in the class whom he had recently taken on a date to shout: "Alex, come back!"

A photographer captured Vraciu jumping from the window, and the stunt subsequently received nationwide media attention. When he landed safely in the waiting tarpaulin and looked up, Vraciu could see that his classmates had rushed to the windows with horrified expressions on their faces, expecting the worse. "My life was different from that point on," he noted, as he received credit for every crazy stunt pulled on the campus. This continued to occur even when he was thousands of miles away as a navy pilot in the Pacific during World War II. When Vraciu returned to the psychology class after his successful practical joke, Fay had all the other students write down what they had witnessed. Vraciu had been maintaining a B grade for the class, but ended up with an A for the course.

The carefree days of Vraciu's early years at DePauw turned serious as Europe became engulfed in another war. Nazi Germany's invasion of Poland on September 1, 1939, had sparked declarations of war from the allied powers, Great Britain and France. After a period of quiet—a time that came to be known as the "phony war"—Germany unleashed its powerful military machine, invading and taking control of Denmark, Holland, and Belgium. France finally surrendered on June 22, 1940.

The bulk of British troops and some French forces had managed to make their way back to England from the beaches of Dunkirk, thanks to the help of hundreds of small ships that had sailed across the English Channel to aid in their rescue. Great Britain now stood alone against Nazi Germany. In a speech before the House of Commons, Prime Minister Winston Churchill, the leader of the British government, vowed to "defend our Island, whatever the cost may be, we shall fight on the beaches . . . we shall never surrender."

In preparation for a possible invasion of Great Britain, the German air force, the Luftwaffe, flew across the English Channel to drop bombs on English cities. Determined pilots from the Royal Air Force took to their Hawker Hurricane and Supermarine Spitfire fighter aircraft to challenge the Luftwaffe's bombers—the Battle of Britain had begun.

The war raging in Europe divided public opinion in the United States. The stunning success of Hitler's Nazi Germany and its brutal treatment of Jews and others who opposed it helped to create much sympathy for England's plight. But there existed in the country a powerful group of isolationists who believed America should not involve itself in the foreign conflict. Famous flier Lindbergh served as a key spokesman for the isolationist America First Committee, formed in 1940 to argue the case against U.S. involvement in the war.

On the DePauw campus, Vraciu noted that people existed in a "horrible limbo at the time." Students were split into those who supported the America First Committee and others who favored aiding England in its fight against Germany. Everyone could sense, remembered Vraciu, that the United States might eventually be dragged into the war. "I decided if we were going to go to war, I would become a fighter pilot," said Vraciu, who was inspired in part by the news he heard over the radio about the Battle of Britain.

First, of course, Vraciu had to learn how to fly. The opportunity came in the summer between his junior and senior year. During the 1930s, several countries in Europe, anticipating the need for trained pilots for military service, had been instructing civilians for the task. In 1938 the United States followed suit by creating the Civilian Pilot Training Program that planned to train twenty thousand civilians a year to provide a potential source for the army air corps, navy, and marines. The federal government funded a program that included seventy-two hours worth of ground school and thirty-five to fifty hours of flight instruction at airports and installations near colleges and universities across the country. By the fall of 1940, approximately seven hundred schools had joined the program. From 1939 to 1944, the CPTP trained more than four hundred thousand pilots.

Vraciu became one of those who learned to fly through the CPTP. At the end of his junior year at DePauw, Vraciu had secured a summer job at Inland Steel. Before he left for home, however, one of his fraternity brothers, John Warner of Muncie, who also had an interest in becoming a pilot, said he would check to see if the CPTP might be offered at Ball State University. "I said, 'Oh, that sounds great,'" Vraciu recalled. "He [Warner] said, 'I'll let you know, I'll give you a call.'" Ball State had such a program and when Vraciu received the call from Warner he was on the bus that night for the more than two-hundred-mile trip to Muncie.

Unfortunately for Warner, his eyes were bad and he did not have the opportunity to take the course. Vraciu passed the initial physical examination, paid a small fee for insurance and textbooks, and began his training. This training included courses on aviation history, air regulations, navigation, meteorology, and the theory of flight. Students also learned how to taxi, take off, and land an airplane, before taking to the air with an instructor to deal with such emergencies as spins and forced landings. Those who qualified would take a solo flight, and then move on to more time in the air on their own.

When he first arrived in Muncie, Vraciu stayed at Warner's home, but soon found room and board at a local restaurant. Vraciu had a busy schedule that summer. He attended ground school in the morning learning the fundamentals of flying and had hands-on experience in a small, two-seat Piper J-3 Cub airplane in the afternoon, or vice versa. In the evening Vraciu worked in the restaurant's kitchen.

Vraciu received his flight training from Larry Hirschinger, whose interest in aviation had been inspired by Lindbergh's historic flight and had been teaching people how to fly at a small airport between Tipton and Elwood. Hirschinger came to Muncie the day after Christmas in 1939 to manage the local airport. He eventually trained more than two thousand pilots for service in the military, all without any serious injuries. Vraciu's abilities impressed Hirschinger, who told him that he possessed a knack for flying. "I didn't have any fears," Vraciu said of his early days in the air. After completing the course, Vraciu received his private pilot's license.

Returning to DePauw for his senior year, Vraciu, like many young college students, expected that America would soon be drawn into the war. A Gallup Poll taken in 1941 revealed that 85 percent of those polled believed the United States would be involved in the war in Europe, with two-thirds in another poll predicting a conflict with Japan. The year before Congress had passed the Selective Service and Training Act, which instituted the first peacetime draft in American history. All men between the ages of twenty-one and thirty had to register with their local draft boards and, if drafted, were to serve for one year in the military.

Before he could be drafted, Vraciu, in the fall of 1940, declared his intention to join the navy and serve as a pilot. "I knew what I wanted by that time," he recalled. "I figured the war was going to grab us. That's why I went in the navy." He completed his studies at DePauw, graduating in June 1941 with a degree in sociology. Before being

Top: Owen Fisher (left) and Dale Fisher talk after a flight for the Civilian Pilot Training Program at the Muncie Airport in 1941. **Above:** Larry Hirschinger, the pilot who trained Vraciu to fly, poses with other members of the coordinating staff for the CPTP in Muncie. The members are: Front row, left to right, Clyde Shockley, Doctor Ralph Noyer, and W. E. Wagoner; back row, left to right, Hirschinger, Robert MacIntyre, Donald Oren, and Lawrence Spearman.

finally called up for service on October 9, Vraciu worked for a few months at Inland Steel. Leaving to join the military, he promised his fellow workers he would come back later and "buzz them" in his navy aircraft—a promise he made sure to keep.

3

OFF THE GROUND

When Alex Vraciu reported to the Glenview Naval Air Station near Chicago, Illinois, to receive his preliminary training as a navy pilot in 1941, he joined a service that had to fight for recognition and respect with the more traditional U.S. Navy. During this era, seapower advocates such as Alfred Thayer Mahan had emphasized the primary role of heavy battleships in decisive engagements between nations' naval forces on the high seas.

That role began to be challenged, however, on the afternoon of November 14, 1910, on the waters near Hampton Roads, Virginia. The conditions were rough and choppy that day as rain squalls threatened the area. Despite the nasty weather, Eugene B. Ely, a daredevil pilot, snapped on his goggles, revved his engine, and started down a wooden platform atop the scout cruiser USS *Birmingham* in a fragile aircraft built by aviation pioneer Glenn Curtiss. After clearing the platform's edge, Ely and his plane nearly crashed into the water. The pilot avoided disaster and, after a five-minute, two-and-a-half-mile journey, landed safely on dry land. Ely had made the first successful flight from a warship.

Excited by his accomplishment, Ely told Captain Washington Chambers, who had been charged with investigating the future of aviation for the navy, that pilots "could light on a ship (as well as takeoff) with little difficulty." John Barry Ryan, the head of the U.S. Aeronautical Reserve and the person who had provided the money to

Dressed in his flight gear, Eugene B. Ely (right) stands in front of his Curtiss Pusher aircraft. At left, Ely becomes the first man to take off from a warship, flying his plane from the USS *Birmingham* (the destroyer USS *Roe* can be seen in the background). Above left, Ely achieves another first when he lands on the deck of the USS *Pennsylvania*. At the top, Ely, is greeted by the commanding officer of the *Pennsylvania*, Captain Charles F. Pond.

build the platform on the *Birmingham*, honored Ely's achievement by awarding him $500 and making him a lieutenant in the reserve.

Just a few months later, on January 18, 1911, Ely achieved another milestone in naval aviation history when he became the first man to land a plane on a ship. Taking off from a horse-racing track near San Francisco, California, Ely landed his Curtiss aircraft on a temporary wooden platform built over the deck of the armored cruiser USS *Pennsylvania*. Hooks had been attached to Ely's landing gear in order to catch a series of twenty-two ropes weighted with sandbags that had been stretched across the deck. Sailors rigged canvas awnings along the sides of the ship to snag the plane in case it veered off course. (These same methods, modified over the years, have become the standard way to capture planes on aircraft carriers of all types.)

After receiving congratulations from his wife and the *Pennsylvania*'s commanding officer, Captain Charles F. Pond, and eating a hearty lunch, Ely climbed back into his plane and took to the skies once again. A delighted Pond described the event as "the most important landing of a bird since the dove flew back to the Ark." The captain indicated to newspaper reporters that aircraft would play important roles in the future in naval warfare and called upon the navy to build "new vessels to serve as floating airfields from which land type aircraft [could] take off and land."

It took several years, however, for the navy to make good on the promise of Ely's groundbreaking flights. In 1919 Great Britain had been the first nation to launch an operational aircraft carrier, the HMS *Hermes*. Three years later, the U.S. Navy converted a coal-carrying cargo ship, the USS *Jupiter*, into its first aircraft carrier, the USS *Langley* (named for aviation pioneer Samuel Pierpont Langley). For many years the *Langley* served as a test bed to train fliers and crews in the intricate

Trainees at the Glenview Naval Air Station received rigorous classroom instruction during their time at the base. "We taught them to fly, to navigate, to communicate, to recognize the enemy and find their way back to the carrier at night and in storms," noted Jack Witten, the station's commander.

operations of flying and landing aircraft at sea until the advent of larger and more powerful aircraft carriers in the U.S. fleet.

The heavy damage inflicted by Japanese forces on the battleships of the American Pacific Fleet at Pearl Harbor on December 7, 1941, placed new emphasis on the role of aircraft carriers in the conflict. These were now the ships that would have to take the fight to the enemy to win the war in the Pacific. Vraciu and the thousands of other young Americans who volunteered to try and become navy pilots were to be trained not only how to fly, but also how to tackle more experienced Japanese pilots in long-distance battles to protect U.S. ships at sea.

When they were not in the classroom or being drilled on the parade ground, those undergoing training at Glenview relaxed with a game of ping pong or swapped stories at the station's post exchange.

Vraciu's memories of those early days of training were of constant "bottlenecks" wherever he went. "Everywhere we went we had to sit around and wait—we didn't have the carriers or the squadrons," he recalled. "But it was a blessing in disguise because I got in more gunnery [practice] and got in more flight time." Naval facilities were unprepared for the crush of novice pilots waiting to be trained. At Glenview following Pearl Harbor, the navy spent more than $12 million to improve the base, including pouring approximately 1.5 million square yards of concrete for new runways and landing mats and constructing airplane hangars, barracks, dining halls, a hospital, recreation hall, and buildings for administration and ground school. By the end of the war in 1945, fifteen thousand carrier pilots had received their training at Glenview.

Early training at Glenview for navy volunteers (those having at least two years of college and between the ages of twenty and twenty-eight) was keyed to weeding out those unsuitable to become pilots. Because of his experience with the Civilian Pilot Training Program, Vraciu had an edge on many of his classmates. "I knew I could fly," he noted, "and that helped a lot."

After completing the course at Glenview, volunteers were either sent to navy bases in Pensacola, Florida, or Corpus Christi, Texas, as aviation cadets for an additional six months of training before being commissioned as ensigns and being assigned to a squadron. Due to the confusion of wartime and the immense numbers of men to be processed, the navy instead sent Vraciu and others who had passed Glenview to the Dallas Naval Air Station for a short time. Vraciu finally ended up at Corpus Christi in early 1942. "We went through a lot of different phases of training before we were declared for one type of airplane or another," he said. For the most part, the instructors were

After completing his training at Glenview, Vraciu (fifth from right, back row, top photo), joined other graduates (seen drilling at the photo to the left) at the Dallas Naval Air Station for a short time. Located on Mountain Creek Lake in southwest Dallas County, Texas, the station grew to more than a 150 acres during the war years.

Top: Lieutenant Butch O'Hare (left) receives congratulations from Lieutenant Commander John S. "Jimmy" Thach after shooting down five Japanese bombers attempting to attack the USS *Lexington*. **Above:** O'Hare sits in the cockpit of his Grumman F4F Wildcat fighter plane, circa spring 1942.

"pretty nice guys," Vraciu remembered. "They knew they had to crank out pilots and you had to be pretty horrible before they'd do something . . . to boot you out of there."

Vraciu had become determined to be a fighter pilot, preferring that to flying either a torpedo plane or a dive-bomber. If the navy had not allowed him to fly fighters, he vowed to leave the program and try his luck with the U.S. Army Air Corps, which had a base in San Antonio, Texas. "I wanted fighters and I told them so," said Vraciu. "I meant it." (The navy later changed its policies and if a cadet did not accept his airplane assignment, he might be reassigned as a seaman second class and sent out for service in the fleet.)

The Hoosier pilot's determination to become a fighter pilot might have been strengthened by a navy flyer who spoke to him and his fellow cadets while at Corpus Christi—Edward "Butch" O'Hare, who had received his country's highest award for conspicuous gallantry in combat, the Medal of Honor. "I remembered how impressed we all were," said Vraciu. "Little did I know then that later I'd be flying on his wing when he got his own squadron."

Born in Saint Louis, Missouri, and a graduate of the U.S. Naval Academy in Annapolis, Maryland, O'Hare made a name for himself while flying with Fighting Squadron 3 aboard the aircraft carrier USS *Lexington*. On February 20, 1942, the *Lexington* came under attack by nine Japanese G4M Mitsubishi bombers, known by the code name "Betty" by American forces. Flying an F4F Wildcat fighter, O'Hare and his wingman, Duff Dufilho, took on the enemy force and shot down five bombers, saving his ship from possible destruction.

After his heroics in the air, O'Hare had to endure being shot at by a trigger-happy member of the *Lexington* crew as he landed on the ship. "Son," O'Hare told the embarrassed sailor, "if you don't stop shooting at me when I got my wheels down, I'm going to have to report you to the gunnery officer." For his actions that day, O'Hare became the first naval aviator to receive the Medal of Honor and was promoted to lieutenant commander.

News of O'Hare's victories came at a time when the United States needed some good news—the war in the Pacific was not going well. Panic had gripped the country, with many citizens on the West Coast fearful of a Japanese invasion. An army general had even warned people in San Francisco that "death and destruction are likely to come to this city at any moment." Fearful that American citizens of Japanese

U.S. NATIONAL ARCHIVES

The British warships HMS *Prince of Wales* (left, front) and HMS *Repulse* (left, behind) maneuver to avoid an air attack from the Japanese. A destroyer, either the HMS *Express* or *Electra*, is seen in the foreground.

descent living on the West Coast might prove to be disloyal, the U.S. government, under Executive Order 9066 signed by President Franklin D. Roosevelt, forced them against their will from their homes and moved more than a hundred thousand to isolated internment camps in such states as California, Idaho, Nevada, Utah, Wyoming, Colorado, and Arkansas.

The hysteria was fueled in part by the rapid advance by Japan's military in the Pacific. After its surprise attack on Pearl Harbor, Japan had run off a series of victories against possessions controlled by the British, Americans, and Dutch. U.S. marines made a spirited defense of Wake Island, repulsing the initial Japanese landing attempt. The American public became enthralled at the brave defense of the tiny island, and a myth grew that when the marines were radioed about what they required, they had responded: "Send us more Japs!" That was by no means a true statement; the marines were in desperate need of supplies, but a relief column of ships turned back, and the Japanese captured the island on December 23, 1941.

More bad news followed. Manila, the capital of the Philippines, fell to the enemy on January 2, 1942, and by March General Douglas MacArthur, commander of the U.S. Army in the Far East, had been ordered to leave the Philippines for Australia. Arriving in a country fearful of invasion by the Japanese, the general known for his tattered cap and corncob pipe made his famous vow: "I came through and I shall return."

The British also suffered, losing such key possessions as Hong Kong and Malay. Two of England's mightiest warships, the battleship HMS *Prince of Wales* and battle cruiser HMS *Repulse*, in an attempt to stop an enemy invasion force headed for Malay, were attacked and sunk by Japanese bombers and torpedo planes on December 10, 1941. They

A U.S. Army Air Corps B-25 Mitchell bomber takes off from USS *Hornet* at the start of the famous Doolittle Raid, April 18, 1942. Note the sailors watching from the signal lamp platform at right.

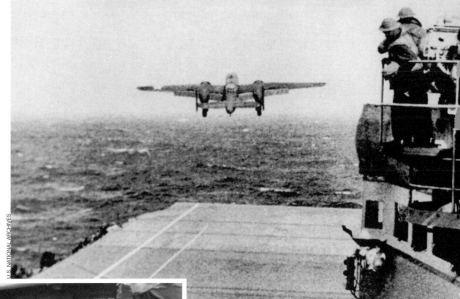

U.S. NATIONAL ARCHIVES

U.S. NAVAL HISTORICAL CENTER

U.S. NATIONAL ARCHIVES

U.S. NAVAL HISTORICAL CENTER

Above: Lieutenant Colonel James Doolittle (left front), leader of the bomber force, and Captain Marc Mitscher, commanding officer of the *Hornet*, pose with a five-hundred-pound bomb and aircrew members while en route to the raid on Japan. **Above, Right:** A B-25B prepares for takeoff from the *Hornet*. The white stripes painted on the flight deck guided the pilot's alignment of his plane's nose and port side wheels. **Below, Right:** Admiral Isoroku Yamamoto of the Imperial Japanese Navy.

were the first capital ships to be sunk solely by an attack from the air while operating on the open seas.

Receiving the news of the disaster the next morning, British Prime Minister Winston Churchill could not believe what he heard. "In all the war, I never received a more direct shock," Churchill recalled "As I turned over and twisted in bed the full horror of the news sank in upon me. There were no British or American ships in the Indian Ocean or the Pacific except the American survivors of Pearl Harbor, who were hastening back to California. Over all this vast expanse of waters Japan was supreme, and we everywhere were weak and naked."

In August 1942 Vraciu earned the gold wings of a navy pilot. At that time, the tide had seemed to turn for the Americans in the Pacific. On April 18 a force of sixteen normally land-based North American B-25 Mitchell bombers led by Lieutenant Colonel James Doolittle had flown off the pitching deck of the aircraft carrier *Hornet* to bomb Tokyo, Japan's capital city. Although the bombers did little damage, the raid boosted morale in the United States and shocked Japanese citizens, who started to doubt, as one of them remembered, that "we were invincible."

Incensed by the Doolittle raid, the Japanese sent a large fleet to capture Midway Island, an American possession located about a thousand miles northwest of Honolulu, Hawaii. In addition to capturing Midway, Japanese Admiral Isoroku Yamamoto hoped to draw out the American fleet for a decisive battle. American Douglas SBD Dauntless dive-bombers, however, shattered Yamamoto's dreams, screaming down to sink four Japanese carriers against the loss of only one American carrier, the *Yorktown*. Japan had been put on the defensive and "the Americans had avenged Pearl Harbor," noted a Japanese government official.

Above: The wreckage left behind of Vraciu's North American SNJ Texan aircraft after he and a passenger bailed out near Lemon Grove, California.
Inset: On the early afternoon of June 6, 1942, Dauntless dive-bombers from USS *Hornet* approach the burning Japanese heavy cruiser *Mikuma* to make another attack during the Battle of Midway.

After receiving his wings from the navy, Vraciu had gone for advanced carrier training at the North Island Naval Air Station at San Diego, California. It was there that Vraciu learned just how dangerous flying could be. His close call came while practicing formation flying in a North American SNJ Texan aircraft on October 14, 1942. Cruising in good weather at an altitude of four thousand feet over Lemon Grove, California, Vraciu was the number two plane in a three-plane division. While practicing his shifting to left echelon position, the number three plane's pilot, W. L. Gleason, lowered his aircraft too soon and his right wingtip and aileron tore into the tail of Vraciu's plane.

The damage was so great to the airplane's elevator and rudder controls that Vraciu could barely manage to control its flight. "I could see I was getting absolutely nowhere," he said. He turned to his passenger, a sailor named F. E. Tyler, who had never flown in an airplane before, and told him to bail out. Vraciu remembered that Tyler barely squeaked out a question, "Jump?" "Yes," Vraciu replied. "Get the hell out of there." (Tyler landed safely, suffering only slight lacerations to his face and forehead.)

After his passenger left, Vraciu at first believed he might be able to make it back to the airfield. The other pilot in the mishap had been able to return his airplane to a safe landing. Realizing the damage was too great for him to return to the base, Vraciu decided to jump. He unfastened his seatbelt and was immediately thrown violently out of the plane, tumbling out of control in the sky. He was barely able to pull his ripcord in time for his parachute to open and swing one turn and half of another before ending in a lemon tree near a farmhouse.

The crippled aircraft Vraciu had flown landed with a tremendous crash close to the farmhouse. The sound startled a pregnant woman in the house so much that she had her baby early, Vraciu remembered.

Vraciu (first from left, back row) and other navy fliers at the Melbourne Naval Air Station in Florida. The navy used the station for gunnery training and more than two thousand pilots received instruction at the station during the war.

When an ambulance arrived at the scene, the doctor told him he was glad to see he was still alive and uninjured, as too many pilots tried to "be a hero and bring the plane back," often crashing and losing their lives in the process. Before returning to the base, Vraciu made sure to pick the biggest lemon from the tree to present to Gleason. "He took it with a weak smile," Vraciu laughed.

The Hoosier pilot suffered another close call when he and other navy pilots flew some Wildcat fighters to open up a new naval air station at Melbourne, Florida, where they received gunnery training and field carrier landing practice. While there, Vraciu and his buddies flew for a part of the day, and spent the rest of the time fishing, golfing, or relaxing on the beach. Another pilot convinced Vraciu that they should engage in a dangerous mock dogfight at night. "I was crazy enough to do it," he recalled.

While the two planes were battling back and forth for position in the dark skies over Florida, the other pilot suddenly turned off all the navigational lights on his airplane. Vraciu stopped the dogfight and turned to look back over his shoulder to see the other aircraft just as its pilot turned on his bright landing lights. This caused Vraciu to become dizzy with vertigo. "I couldn't tell what was up and what was down," he said. Remembering his training, Vraciu ignored the confused signals from his senses and instead concentrated on the gauges in his cockpit that indicated his altitude and airspeed. Using these gauges as his guide, he landed safely back at the base.

Often the greatest challenge that faced a naval aviator early in his career came when he had to qualify by landing and taking off from the pitching deck of an aircraft carrier. Finding the proper place for such an activity proved to be a difficult task for the U.S. Navy. The waters off the coast of California were still under threat from Japanese submarines, and German U-boats prowled the waters just off the East Coast of America. Pilots could simulate landing on a carrier by practicing hitting their marks on the outline of the ship painted on a regular runway, but it could not duplicate the real thing.

Instead of risking its valuable warships, the navy hit upon an ingenious method for training its rookie pilots and the landing signal officers who guided the planes to the deck. The navy purchased two former side-wheel passenger liners, the SS *Seeandbee* and SS *Greater Buffalo*, both of which had cruised the Great Lakes. These coal-powered ships were converted into training aircraft carriers christened the USS *Wolverine* and the USS *Sable*. Pilots flew from the Glenview Naval Air

The USS *Wolverine* makes its way along the waters of Lake Michigan. Many pilots seeking to land on the ship compared the size of its deck to that of a postage stamp.

Station and practiced takeoffs and landings as these unarmed carriers plied the waters of Lake Michigan, far away from any enemy forces.

Training went on seven days a week. After taking off from Glenview, a squadron of trainees rendezvoused at Point Oboe near Wilmette, Illinois, a site easy to distinguish because of the large, domed Baha'i House of Worship located there. To qualify, a pilot had to make eight successful takeoffs and landings from the converted carriers.

Flying a Wildcat fighter, Vraciu made his qualifying takeoffs and landing on the *Wolverine* with no problems. "I took to it pretty quickly," he noted, "showing an early affinity for carrier duty." Vraciu became one of the 17,800 pilots from the navy to qualify on the converted Lake Michigan carriers during the war (another navy flyer to do so was George H. W. Bush, who later served as the country's forty-first president). Vraciu also made good on his promise to say hello to his former friends at the Inland Steel factory in East Chicago by streaking by the plant in his navy aircraft.

Vraciu had more trouble traveling to his next assignment than he ever had on the *Wolverine*. He and a couple of other navy pilots had gone to a Chicago-area car dealer and convinced the owner to let them transport one of his cars to San Diego, where they were to report again to North Island. The novice pilots would take turns driving across the country. Unfortunately, somewhere near Phoenix, Arizona, while Vraciu and another pilot were asleep in the backseat, the person driving took a ninety-degree turn too fast and rolled the car off the road. Luckily, no one was injured in the crash, and the pilots hitched a ride to the naval air station.

At North Island, Vraciu learned that the pilot he had been so impressed with at Corpus Christi—O'Hare—was starting to put together a squadron for eventual service in the Pacific. Chance played a big part in Vraciu being able to join O'Hare's squadron. There was an assignment available on a small escort carrier ferrying fighter aircraft to Guadalcanal, where fierce fighting had been going on between American and Japanese forces for control of this critical island. Vraciu and a friend of his flipped a coin—Vraciu won and joined O'Hare's group at the end of February 1943.

Fighting Squadron 3 (known to its members as "Butch's Boys") left San Diego in June, sailing to the Hawaiian Islands on board the escort carrier the USS *Prince William*. They settled in for further training at the Puunene Naval Air Station on Maui. "He had a very quiet demeanor," Vraciu said of O'Hare, "and he didn't have to say much. We just absorbed what he did say." The commander was a person who led by example, according to Vraciu. Of course, that did not stop O'Hare from chewing someone out if he did something wrong.

O'Hare urged his pilots to always anticipate what might happen next when they were in the air. "This is no drill," he warned them. "We aren't playing funsies. You have to anticipate every move your opponent may make. If you sit there fat, dumb and happy—you're dead." The commander also was exacting in how his pilots flew in formation. Many of the younger members of the squadron tried to get as close as possible to O'Hare to show off their flying skills, but the veteran would just wave them back to what he believed to be the proper place in the flight.

The new squadron commanded by the war hero drew the interest of Merle Miller, a correspondent for *Yank*, a weekly magazine published by and for men and women in the military during the war. In an article titled "What's Butch O'Hare Doing These Days?" Miller reported that most days were routine for the pilots, with four to five hours of flying and games of checkers using Coke-bottle caps for pieces and

Members of Fighting Squadron 3 (later changed to Fighting Squadron 6) sit for a group photograph while in Maui, Hawaii, in 1943. Vraciu is seated in the center of the second row. The group's commander, Butch O'Hare, is seated sixth from the left in the front row.

an occasional hand of poker. "Like everybody else in uniform," wrote Miller, "they complain about the chow and about the shortage of liquor and women. They make bets on how soon the war will end. They emphasize that they want to 'get into it [the fighting].'" When Miller asked about O'Hare's Medal of Honor, one member of the squadron noted that it and the other medals had been "put away for the duration. You can't wear medals on work clothes."

Sensing that Vraciu had promise, O'Hare picked the rookie pilot to fly as his wingman, charged with looking out for his leader during dangerous combat situations. "I think some of the squadron mates were a little envious," Vraciu laughed, "because he selected me for the job." The two men matched their skills against one another by dogfighting in the skies above Hawaii. "I thought I was pretty hot," Vraciu remembered, "but you're smart enough to know you're starting to lose the dogfight to somebody."

With O'Hare getting closer and closer to latching onto the tail of his aircraft, a desperate Vraciu pulled up into the sun—a maneuver that could possibly cause a collision. When the two men landed, according to Vraciu, his commander tried to explain to him "in a nice way that learning how to do certain things was important, but killing both of us at the same time would not help the war effort."

The commander kept a close eye on the development of his young flyers and always expressed concern about their safety. On one occasion, Vraciu expressed an interest in flying the army's Curtiss P-40 Warhawk fighter. Worried about a possible accident in an unfamiliar airplane, O'Hare asked his wingman: "Why do you want to fly it? Just to say you flew it?" Vraciu sheepishly agreed that O'Hare's reasoning was correct, but went ahead and flew the P-40 anyway.

O'Hare taught other lessons to Vraciu as well. These included how to conserve both fuel and ammunition, to fly as close as possible to the enemy before opening fire, to aim at an airplane's vulnerable wing roots (the place where the wings joined the fuselage and where the gas tanks were located), and to always look back over his shoulder for possible enemy planes before starting his dive on a strafing run. "I feel it may have saved my life several times," said Vraciu. "You know, it doesn't hurt to know that you learned it right."

Fighting Squadron 3 was one of the first to receive the navy's newest fighter—the F6F Hellcat. Manufactured by the Grumman Aircraft Corporation, the Hellcat had been designed from the outset to take on and defeat in combat the feared Japanese Zero, which had been the dominant aircraft in the skies above the Pacific. American pilots had been able to counter the Zero's superior abilities by developing such

An aerial view of seven Grumman Hellcat planes in flight. The second largest fighter aircraft of the war (only the Republic P-47 Thunderbolt was larger), the Hellcat proved to be extremely rugged in combat, as well as being easy to repair.

defensive maneuvers as the "Thach Weave," developed by Lieutenant Commander John S. "Jimmy" Thach with O'Hare's assistance, but badly needed an improved fighter if America was to win the war in the Pacific.

The navy had first hoped that they had found a worthy adversary to the Zero with the gull-winged Chance-Vought F4U Corsair. The Corsair, however, was difficult to land on carriers because of problems with its landing gear, but proved to be an effective ground-based aircraft with the U.S. Marine Corps. The navy, however, found what it was looking for with the Hellcat. "The Grumman people had a mutual, long 'love' relationship with the navy over the years," Vraciu noted.

In January 1943 the navy began receiving Hellcats from Grumman. The aircraft came equipped with a powerful Pratt and Whitney two-thousand-horsepower supercharged engine, thick armor plating around the cockpit and engine, a bullet-resistant windscreen, and a rubber-coated, self-sealing fuel tank. The Hellcat was faster than the Zero, could outclimb it, and also outperform the enemy airplane in a dive. In addition, the Hellcat turned out to be a dependable plane and could take substantial damage in combat and still make it back safely to the carrier. One pilot rated the Hellcat a "100 percent better" airplane than its predecessor, the Wildcat.

Vraciu considered the Hellcat as the "perfect carrier plane," as it proved to be a good plane for both veteran and rookie pilots. "It was stable, and it was a beautiful gun platform," he observed. "It would outgun, with the six .50-calibers—three on each wing—the Zero. If you maintained a speed of about 250 knots [approximately 287 miles per hour] and fought them on a vertical plane, then you could handle the Zero. Their stick forces at high speeds were such that they couldn't turn with you, and you could follow them down and get them.

If they're on your tail, you could pull away from them and outturn them and get away." By war's end, 307 pilots had achieved ace status (shooting down five or more enemy planes) flying in a Hellcat.

American pilots were also aided in their efforts against the lethal Zero by a chance find. During the Battle of Midway, the Japanese had attacked and occupied a part (Attu, Agattu, and Kiska islands) of the Aleutians, a chain of nearly three hundred islands near what was then the U.S. territory of Alaska. A Japanese pilot had attempted to make an emergency landing on Akutan Island, but became stuck in a bog. American forces discovered the plane on July 10, 1942, and recovered it and took it to the North Island Naval Air Station at San Diego, California.

Navy crews worked night and day to repair the Zero so it could be flown again. Once it was ready, a navy pilot, Lieutenant Commander Eddie Sanders, tested the Zero's performance on numerous flights, found out its strengths, and discovered several weaknesses. The results were shared, and the navy developed tactics for its pilots to use when dogfighting the Zero.

In July 1943 O'Hare's squadron had its number changed, to Fighting Squadron 6, but the commander made sure to keep for his flyers the famous Felix the Cat cartoon-figure emblem he had been known for throughout his career. Soon, Vraciu and his fellow aviators would test their training and new Hellcat aircraft in direct competition against the Japanese. They also inaugurated into combat a new type of aircraft carrier—the *Independence* class—that would become a valuable contributor to America's rise to dominance in the Pacific conflict.

4

THE FAST CARRIERS

The year 1943 saw the U.S. Navy begin to take the offensive in the war in the Pacific. To defeat the Japanese Empire, the navy relied on fast task forces built around its large, modern *Essex*-class aircraft carriers that could carry thirty-six fighters, thirty-six dive bombers, and eighteen torpedo planes. These ships (classified as CVs by the navy) were fast, traveling at a speed of thirty-three knots (about thirty-eight miles per hour) and bristled with advanced communication gear and radar to aid in detecting the enemy.

The carriers and their crews of 360 officers and 3,088 enlisted men were protected by antiaircraft fire provided by a ring of battleships, cruisers, and destroyers and were rugged—none were sunk by the enemy during the war. Because of fears that these new carriers would not be available for service until 1944, however, the navy, with a nudge from President Franklin D. Roosevelt, converted what were to be cruiser warships into *Independence*-class light carriers.

Although they were built with short, narrow flight decks upon which aircraft could operate, the *Independence*-class carriers (classified as CVLs) were fast enough to keep up with the larger *Essex*-class vessels. "Once you learned to fly off of, and land, on one of those," said Alex Vraciu, who had experience sailing onboard the light carriers, "you could land on anything." Another navy pilot compared landing on these ships to "hitting a splinter with a bolt of lightning." Still, this class of carrier was much preferred over the even smaller and slower

escort carriers (CVEs), which were nicknamed by their crews as "Combustible, Vulnerable and Expendable."

Because of their smaller size (the ship had a crew of 1,569 men), the *Independence* class initially carried only twelve Hellcat fighters and nine torpedo planes and nine dive bombers. As the war progressed, more fighters were added and the number of dive-bombers and torpedo planes carried were reduced.

The fast carrier task forces became the knife with which the United States slashed into the Japanese. These lethal armadas could remain operating at sea for seventy days thanks to the efforts of oilers that refueled the ships on the go and supply ships that replenished stocks of ammunition and food, as well as bringing mail from home and the latest movies from Hollywood for the entertainment-starved sailors and airmen.

In July 1943 a new light aircraft carrier, the USS *Independence*, sailed into Pearl Harbor. This was the ship that took Vraciu and other greenhorn members of Fighting Squadron 6 on their first combat

U.S. NATIONAL ARCHIVES

Opposite: The USS *Independence* steams in San Francisco Bay, California, on July 15, 1943. On the ship's deck are nine scout bombers and nine torpedo planes. Left: The *Independence* hauls in its anchor while off the Mare Island Navy Shipyard.

mission to test out the new American planes and ships against the Japanese. Things did not begin well—rookie flight crews onboard had problems and there were some mishaps involving the pilots. Unfortunately, these early difficulties caused some to begin to refer to the *Independence* as the *Evil I*. Crew members, however, preferred to remember a motto provided by one of the ship's captains: "The difficult we do immediately; . . . the impossible takes a little longer."

In late August, the *Independence*, joined by the carriers *Yorktown* and *Essex*, along with other ships, including the new battleship USS *Indiana*, left Hawaii to strike the Japanese base on tiny Marcus Island. Located a thousand miles east of Tokyo, the coral island held an airfield and approximately four thousand Japanese soldiers. Organized as Task Force 15, the American fleet, under the overall command of Rear Admiral Charles A. Pownall, was set to launch a dawn attack on the island. Vraciu called the mission "a diversionary raid to scare the Japanese. If we could hit Marcus, they would have to consider pulling back some of their strength down south [in the Pacific]."

Launching missions from an aircraft carrier involved a swarm of activity on and below the flight deck. Pilots were awakened early in the morning from their cramped quarters in the carrier's interior and put on their khaki flying suits and cotton helmets with leather earphone covers and clear goggles, buckled on their inflatable Mae West life vests (named in honor of the buxom Hollywood actress), strapped on their parachutes, stowed their survival knives in their proper position, and placed in their shoulder holsters a .38-caliber revolver or .45-caliber pistol in case they had to bail out and defend themselves against the enemy.

Vraciu remembered that the cooks in the ship's galley always seemed to feed the pilots a breakfast of a small steak and eggs. "You

Above: Ordnancemen work on bombs while surrounded by F6F-3 Hellcat fighters parked on an aircraft carrier's hanger deck. In the background, other crewmen watch a movie. **Left:** Pilots on an aircraft carrier somewhere in the Pacific Ocean prepare for a mission in their ready room.

may drink a lot of coffee," he noted, "but somehow you dehydrate so much in the air anyway, that kind of climate out there, it was kind of warmish anyway. You always come back [soaking] wet from the flight." The pilots would then gather together in the air-conditioned ready rooms to be briefed by their air group commander on what kind of opposition they might face and what was expected from them to fulfill their mission.

While the pilots prepared for their flight, out on the deck sailors performed a ballet of sorts to get the fighters, bombers, and torpedo planes ready. Officers on the bridge barked out orders to steer the ship into the wind to aid in launching the planes. Each member of the crew wore color-coded uniforms and helmets to distinguish himself on the crowded flight deck made from wood from Oregon pine or Douglas fir. Ordnancemen in red shirts loaded ammunition and bombs on the aircraft while yellow-shirted plane directors made sure crews placed the planes in the proper position for launch. Watching over all this frenzied activity were firefighters, nicknamed "Hot Pappas," clad in fireproof silver suits and prepared to handle any emergencies.

On missions such as the one at Marcus, the larger carriers were given the chance to make the main attack on the objective. Pilots who flew from smaller carriers such as the *Independence* were often asked to provide a combat air patrol to protect the fleet from any counterattack by the enemy. If threats were detected by the fleet's radar, fighter direction officers (FDOs) in the ship's combat information center could tell if the "bogies" might be a threat through Identification, Friend, or Foe (IFF) transponders installed in each American plane. If the FDO determined the inbound aircraft were hostile, he would radio the enemy's direction so pilots could intercept the threat.

Such patrols could mean action if Japanese planes were eager to try their luck against U.S. ships, but most of the time Vraciu found them "boring." It meant that Hellcat pilots spent hours at a time in an often hot and uncomfortable cockpit. "You'd just bore holes in the sky, and then they'd call you down and land," he remembered. "But they needed them, I know. You took your turns. It evened off."

During the raid on Marcus, Vraciu did have an opportunity, as Butch O'Hare's wingman, to make a strafing run on Japanese installations using the Hellcat's heavy punch of six .50-caliber machine guns. "Strictly go in, strafe, burn planes if there were planes on the runway," he noted. "But if somebody else got there ahead of you, generally the planes would all be burned, so you'd strafe a building, revetments [barricades], or some gun emplacement. Then you'd scoot across and pull up and maybe do a second or third run."

These strafing runs could be dangerous for any pilot, as Japanese antiaircraft crews fired away furiously at the attacking planes. "You had to learn to respect them because you were just a statistic," Vraciu said, "and eventually they were going to get you if you kept doing it. I went down low and paid the penalty for it a few times. But that's when you do the most damage to them." He estimated that 90 percent of American planes hit by the enemy during the war were hit by ground fire. If they were honest, he added, most pilots would "tell you they don't like strafing. They do it because they have no choice. They'd rather have the air action because we figured we could handle ourselves in the air."

Vraciu and O'Hare survived their strafing run on the island with no damage. On the way back to the *Independence*, the Americans came across a small Japanese supply ship that had survived numerous attacks throughout the day and still remained afloat. Hoping to finally destroy what seemed like an unsinkable vessel, called *No. 15 Jitai Maru*, the fighters under O'Hare's command made a couple of passes, firing their machine guns at the damaged craft. A frustrated Vraciu, determined to finish off the *Jitai Maru*, peeled off ahead of O'Hare and made a third run at the ship (a breach in flight discipline that he later "caught hell" for from his commander).

As the six guns on Vraciu's Hellcat clattered away at the ship, it suddenly exploded and went down to the bottom of the ocean. For years, Vraciu believed he had been responsible for the "unsinkable" vessel finally going down. Later, he learned that a pilot from the *Yorktown* flying a Grumman TBF Avenger had dropped its load of four five-hundred-pound bombs on the target, breaking the craft into two pieces. "To this day," Vraciu said, "I still find it hard to believe that anybody else hit it."

The raid was a success, with most of the major Japanese installations on Marcus destroyed by the more than a hundred tons of bombs dropped by the Americans. The United States lost three aircraft during the attacks. Tired pilots heading home, however, were not out of danger just yet. Landing a Hellcat on the deck of a carrier could be a tricky proposition even in good weather. As he approached the carrier, the pilot's eyes turned their attention to one of the most important men on the ship—the landing signal officer (LSO).

Standing on the ship's stern (rear) in front of a canvas screen that helped make him more visible, the LSO used color-coded paddles to signal the pilot if he was on course for a safe landing. If for any reason the LSO saw that an approaching aircraft was out of position, he waved his paddles wildly over his head to signal a pilot to abort the landing and try again. Sometimes a damaged airplane did not have the time for

Landing Signal Officer R. J. Grant from the USS *Enterprise* guides in a Hellcat fighter during flight operations on March 13, 1945.

(Left to right) Vraciu, O'Hare, Sy Mendenhall, and Willie Callan prepare for action on the *Independence*, September 6, 1943. Notice the squadron's designation and date inscribed on the plane's propeller.

another approach, and the LSO and other crew members near him had to quickly dive out of the way into a nearby protected catwalk.

Once they were safely aboard their carrier, pilots had time to tell what had happened while they were in the air to the ship's intelligence officers and, perhaps, take a shot of "medicinal alcohol" from the medical officer. To help relax after a long day flying, the pilots played bridge or a card game known as acey-deucey (sometimes called In Between, where players bet on whether a card dealt from the deck will fall numerically in between the value of two cards placed face up). "We slept a lot in between times," added Vraciu. "That was because you did things in concentrated periods during combat, so . . . you just caught up on your sleep, and whatever other activities you missed out on."

Some of the other crew members looked on the lives of pilots with envy, believing they were pampered. Vraciu pointed out, however, that the pilots were often on standby, ready to fly missions at a moment's notice when enemy planes were sighted. This caused them to be on "adrenalin . . . all the time in the forward [combat] area. You're getting up at all crazy hours. You're eating crazy." They needed to relax whenever possible to relieve the buildup of stress.

If pilots had any time available between missions, they went up on deck and stood on what Vraciu called "vulture's row" to see how others in the squadron might be handling their takeoffs and landings. "Then if somebody does something stupid," he said, "you always have something you can rib him [with] when he gets back in the ready room. It's [a] friendly rivalry." The flight deck, however, was always a potentially dangerous place to be. Even if a pilot landed safely, he could be sitting in his aircraft, minding his own business, and be killed when another plane crashed into his after bouncing over the safety barrier meant to stop him. "You can't believe some of the sights that you see and the things that could happen," Vraciu recalled.

The Marcus Island task force returned to Hawaii, and Vraciu endured three or four "dull" weeks waiting for the squadron's next mission. "There just wasn't any action," he remembered. "We were out there to win that war in a hurry . . . and we just weren't getting at them [the Japanese]. But we *didn't* have the carriers." That changed with time, as more and more of the new *Essex-* and *Independence*-class carriers made their way to the Pacific.

In early October 1943 the *Independence,* joined by two other light carriers and three *Essex*-class ships, departed Hawaii for another raid on a Japanese-held island. The fast carriers were assigned to hit Wake Island, the location of the heroic defense by the U.S. Marine Corps earlier in the war. The navy planes hoped by striking at dawn that they could catch the Japanese defenders napping and knock out the airfield and any enemy planes they encountered. Meanwhile, a force of destroyers and cruisers shelled the island.

For Vraciu, the mission marked his first air-to-air action in his young combat career. "Action came slowly," he said, "but it kept building up." With O'Hare as his commanding officer, Vraciu always seemed to be the in thick of things. "If anybody was going to go out [on a mission], it would be us," said Vraciu. "I was just that way—I was lucky. I call it luck, naturally; after all, a fighter pilot wants to be where the action is."

As Vraciu flew his Hellcat as second section leader of O'Hare's four-plane division assigned to fly cover for the cruisers and destroyers, the group received word that three Zero fighters were heading for Wake. O'Hare was the first person to catch sight of the Japanese, who were flying in a V-formation. Because his radio was not working, Vraciu had to keep his eyes on O'Hare. "I could tell by the way Butch was flying that something was happening," said Vraciu. While O'Hare went after the Zero on the outside of the vee of three planes, Vraciu attacked the one on the inside.

O'Hare was destroying his opponent when Vraciu, for the first time, fired his weapons at an enemy plane in the air. His machine guns hit the target and the Zero began to burn furiously (because Japanese planes lacked armor plating and self-sealing fuel tanks, they caught on fire easily when hit). "I got the Zero wingman on the right, and it felt damned good," Vraciu said of his first kill. "I practically flew through the pieces [of the enemy aircraft]." In the heat of the dogfight, Vraciu looked around and noticed that O'Hare had disappeared below the cloud layer with his wingman (he later learned the American duo had spotted other enemy planes and had gone after them).

Blessed with excellent vision, Vraciu observed out of the corner of his eye the lead Zero that had escaped the initial melee and landed on Wake had skittered off the runway. The enemy pilot then leaped from his cockpit and ran for safety to the nearest foxhole. "I thought, 'I'm going to go down and strafe that sucker!'" Vraciu remembered. He did so, and the bullets from his guns made the Zero catch on fire.

In the course of doing some evasive maneuvers to avoid any possible antiaircraft fire, Vraciu noticed a twin-engine G4M Mitsubishi Betty bomber parked near the runway. He pulled his Hellcat around and, with his wingman Willie Callan, went back and destroyed the aircraft. The two men made it safely back to the *Independence*, where questions awaited. "I caught a little hell, when I got back, for not going below the cloud with Butch, but I didn't see him go below," Vraciu said. "But I learned that this is what can happen in combat. Sometimes there is separation, but you learn a lesson."

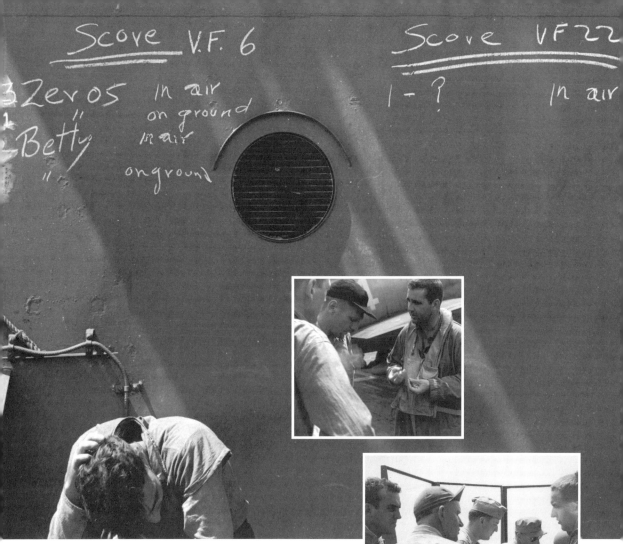

Score V.F. 6

3 Zeros In air
" on ground
2 Betty In air
" on ground

Score VF 22

1 - ?   In air

The crew on the *Independence* used chalk to mark the success of their aircrew during the raid on Wake Island. **Inset, Above:** O'Hare talks about the Wake mission with Chief Willie Williams. **Inset, Right:** Vraciu (pictured at far right) offers his views on the Wake mission to officers on the *Independence*.

In addition to a conference with O'Hare, Vraciu, after landing his Hellcat back on the *Independence*, gave an account of the raid to senior naval officers on the flattop, including its captain, R. L. Johnson. Results of the mission for Fighting Squadron 6 (the number of enemy planes shot down) were written in chalk on the superstructure of the ship's island for all to see. "It helps the ship's crew . . . because when they visualize what they're out there for—that is, to hit the enemy— vicariously they get the same thrill that we got," Vraciu recalled.

The war between the Japanese and Americans in the Pacific was one waged with little or no mercy on either side. The Japanese military viewed surrendering as dishonorable, and their soldiers often fought to the death. They sometimes even pretended to be dead or injured before rising up and trying to kill as many Americans as possible. U.S. airmen and troops who became prisoners of war were treated harshly by the Japanese, suffering beatings and other severe punishments, as well as a lack of proper food and water.

Stories of POW abuse were passed from soldier to soldier, especially the story of the violence committed by the Japanese against the Americans who had surrendered following the fall of the Philippines— what became known as the infamous Bataan Death March. These atrocities, combined with outrage over the sneak attack on Pearl Harbor and sometimes racial hatred, fueled a take-no-prisoners approach by American ground troops as they battled the Japanese on the hostile terrain of Pacific islands.

The ferocity of the fighting led to atrocities on both sides. Japanese soldiers mutilated the bodies of U.S. troops and left them for their comrades to find. They also regularly shot at army medics and navy corpsmen attempting to aid wounded men on the battlefield. Although prohibited under military law, a few American soldiers knocked

Phoenix war worker Natalie Nickerson attempts to write her U.S. Navy boyfriend a thank-you note for sending her a Japanese soldier's skull he had gathered as a souvenir while fighting in New Guinea.

gold teeth from enemy corpses and passed along instructions in the "cooking and scraping of the heads of Japanese to prepare the skulls for souvenirs." A photograph in a May 1944 issue of *Life* magazine showed an American girl staring at a Japanese skull sent to her by her boyfriend, a lieutenant in the navy. (Readers of the magazine were outraged—one who wrote a letter to *Life* called the souvenir "revolting and horrible"— and military officials formally reprimanded the officer.)

The war in the air was just as deadly, but not, perhaps, as personal, Vraciu noted, as the one being waged on the ground. A pilot could see that his actions were causing the death of a fellow human being, but every enemy he shot down "is one less that someone is going to have to contend with later," he added. "[It] sounds strange in peacetime to talk about shooting someone down," Vraciu reflected many years after his time in combat. "That was our job. That is what we were trained to do. You can't be squeamish about the thing or you don't belong in a cockpit of that kind of an airplane unless you get that urge to shoot a guy down. That's what you are trained to do. Nobody ever told you it was going to be an easy job."

The raid on Wake Island marked the last mission shared by O'Hare and Vraciu. Upon the *Independence*'s return to Hawaii on October 11, O'Hare received news that he had been promoted to command of a carrier air group (fighters, bombers, and torpedo planes) on the USS *Enterprise*, which meant that he had to leave Fighting Squadron 6. "Everybody feels very badly about losing him—he was very popular with the pilots," a member of the squadron wrote in his diary upon O'Hare's departure.

Vraciu had little time to miss his former commander as he and the other members of the squadron prepared for an attack on one of Japan's main bases in the South Pacific—Rabaul, located on the island of New

Britain northeast of New Guinea in the South Pacific. By 1943 there were more than a hundred thousand Japanese troops on Rabaul, and the base included airfields and port facilities for enemy ships. Vraciu noted that the Japanese had "placed a lot of their carrier pilots ashore there to aid in defense of this offensive base." To reduce the threat posed by the base on Allied operations in the area, the *Independence*, joined by the flattops *Essex*, *Saratoga*, *Princeton*, and *Bunker Hill*, launched a series of strikes against Rabaul on November 11.

Part of Fighting Squadron 6's job on the raid was to escort a group of bombers and protect them from enemy fighters, as well as strafing any ships that were in the harbor. "Off to the side there were plenty of Zeroes, but they were trying to entice you away from escorting, which, of course, we wouldn't do," said Vraciu. He also participated in a combat air patrol in the afternoon where there were a number of threats from Japanese aircraft, but Vraciu "never fired a shot because their planes had already been shot down by our other fighters that earlier had been put on them. A *most* frustrating hop [mission]."

In November Vraciu readied to support Operation Galvanic, whose objective was to quickly seize two small atolls in the Gilbert Island chain: Makin and Tarawa. Plans had the army's Twenty-seventh Infantry Division tackling the Japanese garrison on Makin, while the Second Marine Division received the Tarawa assignment. The marines hoped to clear the heavily defended island of Japanese forces under the command of Rear Admiral Keiji Shibasaki and secure its vital airfield. The Japanese commander had boasted to his approximately 4,800 troops that "a million men couldn't take Tarawa in 100 years." Once the Gilberts had been cleared of the enemy, plans called to use the newly won territory as a jumping-off point for operations to capture Japanese bases in the Marshall and the Mariana islands.

Vraciu had a memorable start to his part in the campaign on a pre-dawn takeoff from the *Independence* on November 18. The squadron was on its way to the target when its new commanding officer decided to test his machine guns. "It was a pitch-dark night, and it shook the hell out of everybody in the division because we never used to do that, *especially* at night," said Vraciu. "I think we all got our first few gray hairs on that [mission]. We thought we were surrounded when we saw those six .50 calibers fire with the tracers and all."

On November 20 as the marines stormed ashore to wrest control of Tarawa from its defenders, Vraciu flew a combat air patrol mission for the fleet. He noticed a Japanese Betty bomber attempting to flee the area by flying low over the water. Since Vraciu had the fastest plane, he was able to catch up to the retreating enemy and open fire. "Somewhere, in my first burst I must have gotten the tail gunner, because I didn't see his cannon shooting 20-millimeter shells," Vraciu said. He learned to respect the tail gunner on the Betty and later learned how to avoid his fire by practicing full deflection runs against other American aircraft as he flew the squadron mail back and forth between the various island bases in Hawaii.

As Vraciu celebrated his second aerial victory, the marines were paying a terrible price to capture the two-mile-long island. "They were too optimistic," one navy flier said of the aerial attacks on the island. "From the aviation point of view, they thought they had just beaten the place to death, that there were probably very few living Japs there, that they were just going to walk ashore and take over, because they'd really pounded it with airplanes, bombs, strafing and those battleships and cruisers pounding away."

The Japanese were sheltered from these attacks, however, in fortified pillboxes, blockhouses, and bunkers around the island. They had prepared heavy antiboat guns, howitzers, mortars, machine guns, and rifles to deliver murderous fire on the advancing Americans. "The bullets were pouring at us like a sheet of rain," remembered one private. For a time, it seemed as if the marines would be thrown back into the sea. War correspondent Robert Sherrod, who wrote a best-selling book on the fighting, said that it was the "only battle which I ever thought we were going to lose."

The Second Marine Division sustained high casualties in winning the first major amphibious operation in the Pacific to be met with organized opposition on the beachhead. More than a thousand marines were killed and approximately 2,300 were wounded. Of the approximately 4,800 Japanese troops, only seventeen were captured alive. The ferocity of the fighting, and the photographs of American dead littering the beaches that were released for publication, shocked a complacent American public that had "never been led to expect anything but an easy war," noted Sherrod.

The American fleet protecting the invasion also came under intense enemy attack. A large group of Betty bombers, armed with torpedoes, swooped down on the *Independence* on the afternoon of November 20. "Some of us were up on the flight deck at the time as the shooting

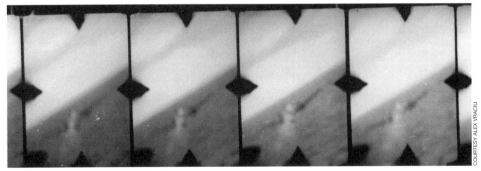

COURTESY ALEX VRACIU

A series of photos from Vraciu's gun camera captures the destruction of a Japanese Betty bomber near Tarawa.

Above: Dead U.S. Marines litter the shore after the Battle of Tarawa. One correspondent noted what he saw on the island was "one of the greatest works of devastation wrought by man."
Right: A marine uses the slim protection of a blasted palm tree on Tarawa to pick off any enemy out in the open.

started," Vraciu said. "Someone said they had spotted a periscope—maybe a submarine was guiding the Bettys. Suddenly, enemy planes were seen making runs down low on the water, and our AA [antiaircraft] fire intensified. At that point, we felt it prudent to go back down to the ready room."

Although gunners on the *Independence* shot down six of the attackers, one launched a torpedo that hit near the ship's stern on the starboard (right) side. "All of a sudden, we felt this BOOM!" Vraciu remembered. Damage-control teams saved the ship, but it still was injured enough that it had to steam to the American-held Funafuti Atoll in the Ellice Islands, seven hundred miles away, for repairs. Because the flattop leaked oil from the torpedo hit, a cruiser had to follow the ship all the way to cut through the slick so the Japanese would not be aware of how badly the *Independence* had been hurt. "Fortunately," said Vraciu, "we weren't hit by any follow-up air attacks."

After several days at Funafuti, Fighting Squadron 6's twelve Hellcats were ordered off the ship to fly to Tarawa and await further orders. After several days on Tarawa, they learned what carrier they would be transferred to (they ended up on the *Essex*). While on the island, Vraciu had a firsthand look at the grave battle that had taken place there and the ugliness of the conflict. Some Japanese still remained alive, hiding in caves, and shooting went on from time to time. The pilots were supposed to sleep in their planes overnight, but because of the gunfire decided instead to huddle in a tent as low as they could get to avoid being hit by a stray bullet.

During the day, Vraciu roamed around the area. He received warnings from troops on Tarawa not to touch anything, as it might have been booby-trapped by the enemy. "You'd see bodies floating on the beach and then you finally got to see . . . what they [the marines] had to face," Vraciu said. The navy pilot also became familiar with the gruesome practice whereby some American troops knocked out the gold teeth from the mouths of deceased Japanese soldiers. One soldier gave Vraciu a gold tooth as a souvenir, and he had a dentist on the *Essex* clean it and drill a hole through it so he could hang it on a gold necklace. He later gave the necklace to his niece when he returned for a visit back in the United States. "Are we ghoulish, or are we not?" asked Vraciu.

When Vraciu reported to the *Essex*, he received some tragic news. His mentor, Butch O'Hare, had been killed—information that quickly passed among the American fleet. O'Hare had been involved on the *Enterprise* in developing night-fighting aircraft teams to protect American ships from the increasing number of Japanese attacks during the evening hours. Vraciu noted that the attacks and response by the fleet kept everyone awake and compared it to the "Fourth of July every night, just about."

While pioneering the night-fighting concept on the evening of November 26, O'Hare and his Hellcat were caught in the crossfire between the Americans and a Japanese Betty bomber that had inadvertently rendezvoused with them. It seemed likely that the Betty shot down the Hellcat. No trace of O'Hare or his airplane was ever found. (On September 19, 1949, Chicago renamed its Orchard Depot Airport to O'Hare International Airport to honor the late navy pilot.)

The loss of his mentor caused Vraciu to make a promise that he shared with his wingman at the time, Willie Callan. "I'm going to get ten of those bastards! Ten Bettys!" Vraciu vowed. O'Hare's death at the hand of the Japanese, combined with his still-fresh outrage about the attack on Pearl Harbor, became the greatest motivators for Vraciu during the rest of the war and why he preferred to place himself at risk rather than to be safely back home. "I'd rather be in combat," he said.

By the end of January 1944, Vraciu had left the *Essex* for a berth on the USS *Intrepid*, an *Essex*-class flattop under the command of Captain Thomas Sprague. For his first mission on the *Intrepid*, Vraciu and his mates from Fighting Squadron 6 sailed from Hawaii with the carriers *Cabot* and *Essex* as part of the American effort to capture the Marshall Islands, codenamed Operation Flintlock. Plans called for the army's veteran Seventh Infantry Division to attack Kwajalein Island (home to the Japanese naval base) in the south, while the untried Fourth Marine Division hit the beaches at Roi (location of the Japanese airfield) and Namur islands in the north.

Vraciu's first opportunity for action came at about ten in the morning on January 29, 1944, during a combat air patrol over the airfield on Roi. When Vraciu arrived over the airfield in his Hellcat, he did not see any enemy planes airborne, so he and his wingman, Tom Hall, prepared to strafe parked Japanese aircraft. Vraciu had spotted a "nice, large, fat transport" plane sitting on the ground, signaled to Hall to attack the airstrip, and had started his dive when all of a sudden he saw a group of Betty bombers flying low over the field. "I remember thinking, 'My prayers are being answered,'" Vraciu recalled.

Maneuvering into the perfect flying position, Vraciu began firing at the first Betty at a range of about three hundred yards. "Perhaps I was a little anxious. But I just seemed right, and I had the perfect shot," he noted. "I barely touched the trigger, and he [the enemy plane] started flaming around the starboard wing root and almost immediately crashed into the sea."

Looking ahead, Vraciu noticed another Betty at an altitude of three hundred feet. The Japanese pilot lowered down to a hundred feet, but could not escape his American foe. "On my first burst the port engine and wing exploded, and the Betty crashed into the lagoon," said Vraciu. "In retrospect—and I don't know exactly when—I probably caught a round in my hydraulic system from his tail-gunner because it affected my ability to fire at the next plane."

Once again glancing ahead, Vraciu could see two more Betty bombers. He headed for the nearest plane while Hall pursued the one farther away. The Betty sped away low over the water hoping to escape the same fate that had befallen his comrades. Being careful not to position his plane in line with the bomber's dangerous 20-millimeter cannon in its tail section, Vraciu made one pass without any visible effect; only one of his guns worked. "I'd get out one or two rounds, and the firing would stop," he said. "It was exasperating for me because I could see his damned tracers heading my way practically each time I made a pass. But I didn't want him to get away."

Finally, after Vraciu made about seven or eight passes at the Betty, it nosed toward the sea and crashed from an altitude of about eighty feet. Vraciu believed that one of his shots must have hit the pilot, causing the Betty to crash. By shooting down three Japanese planes on that day, Vraciu had reached five kills in all, catapulting him to a status every pilot strove for—to be an ace. "They were all Bettys, and that made me feel good—*really* good!" Vraciu said of the combat that day. "I thought, 'Boy! Okay! Good start on my vow! But let's hope we run into a lot more of those on the way.'"

Vraciu had little time to celebrate his victories and ace achievement—an accident onboard the *Intrepid* the very next day robbed him of his wingman. As he prepared to be launched off the carrier on another mission to Kwajalein, Vraciu watched as Hall took off ahead of him, thundered down the deck, and tried to gain altitude. "His left wheel seemed to hit a stanchion off the port bow . . . and his belly tank [a reservoir that carried extra fuel] blew up in the collision," Vraciu said. "His plane ended up in a big fireball off the port side."

Hall would not be the last of the squadron to give his life. More losses were expected as the Americans advanced through the Pacific and faced heavily fortified Japanese bases. Vraciu and his squadron's next target—the Truk Atoll in the Caroline Islands—was viewed by some in command as the "Gibraltar of the Pacific," as it stood as an operating base for the Imperial Japanese Navy's Combined Fleet and served as an important base for the enemy's airfields on Eten, Moen, and Param islands. "Its essential strength," naval historian Samuel Eliot Morison said of Truk, "was given by nature. Naval gunfire from outside the reef could reach neither the islands nor the fleet anchorage in the lagoon. But air power could."

U.S. Navy planners hoped that a strike by carrier aircraft would prevent the Japanese at Truk from offering any support for the upcoming invasion of Eniwetok Atoll in the Marshall Islands. Task Force 58 led by Vice Admiral Marc Mitscher included five large carriers (*Bunker Hill, Enterprise, Essex, Intrepid,* and *Yorktown*) and four light carriers. The attack, code-named Operation Hailstone, was set to begin on February 17, 1944.

Navy officials had initially been worried about the operation, as Mitscher admitted that all he knew about Truk came from his reading of the *National Geographic.* "It was an unknown—[a] big unknown— bastion," recalled Vraciu, who added that many in the fleet were apprehensive about the mission. One navy pilot noted that when he heard the announcement over his ship's loudspeakers that the fleet planned on striking Truk, his "first instinct was to jump overboard."

The Truk attack plan offered a unique opportunity for Hellcat pilots. Instead of escorting bombers to hit the airfields, during the first day of the operation seventy-two fighters from five different carriers were charged with the task of taking control of the air by destroying as many of the enemy as possible, either in the air or on the ground. Because he served on one of the large carriers (the *Intrepid*), Vraciu was assured of "a bigger piece of the action."

The American fighters arrived over their objective just before sunrise on February 17 and began to circle in preparation for strafing attacks on the airfield located on Moen Island in the atoll. Although the Japanese were able to place an impressive amount of antiaircraft fire into the sky, it hit wide of the mark. Vraciu and his wingman, Ensign Lou Little, were the last two in a group of twelve planes from Fighting Squadron 6 off the *Intrepid* that had already begun their dives on the field to blast away at parked aircraft. Remembering what he had been taught by O'Hare, however, Vraciu decided to look back over his shoulder before he dove on the target. "It was a good thing I did," he remembered. "It may have saved a few of our lives."

Vraciu observed that a group of enemy Zeroes were set to pounce on the unsuspecting Americans. "One was already starting to fire," he remembered. "I could see the twinkle of his guns." After warning his fellow pilots, Vraciu and Little turned their Hellcats around and fired at the leading Zero, causing him to break off his attack and dive away. "From that time on, there were enemy planes all around our Hellcats," Vraciu said. "The action was wild and almost unbelievable at times." He called the subsequent battle the wildest of his combat career with so much confusion that one Hellcat fired by mistake on another Hellcat, shooting it down in the process (the pilot successfully bailed out). He also noticed that some of the Japanese pilots seemed to be wearing their pajamas instead of their usual flight suits—the Americans had apparently surprised them with their attack.

Working with Little and another American airman, Vraciu was able to maneuver the enemy into a position where he could go on the offensive. "We noticed that the Japanese weren't reluctant to attack, but once they were cornered, they'd dive steeply toward the water or cloud cover," he said. "We began to follow them down."

Using the speed and power of his Hellcat, Vraciu shot down three of the enemy, all of which crashed into the water. "Once I got on their tail," he said, "I didn't let go." As the Hellcats regrouped for the return to their carriers, Vraciu spied another Zero trying to hide in the clouds. The enemy aircraft did its best to escape, but Vraciu climbed his plane into the sun, leading the Japanese pilot to believe his opponent had given up the chase and left the area. "When I came down on him for the last time, from five o'clock above, he never knew what hit him, I'm sure," Vraciu said. "His wing tank and cockpit exploded."

The action over Truk raised Vraciu's total victories in the air to nine enemy planes shot down. He had a chance to down another Zero, but gave the opportunity and credit for the kill to Little. "A good wingman often doesn't get all the action or credit that he deserves," Vraciu explained, "serving in the role that he does." In addition to the morning mission, he had two other flights that day, spending a total of eight-and-a-half hours in the air. One mission involved flying escort for a group of bombers hitting Japanese ships just north of Truk. Vraciu and other navy pilots spotted an enemy cruiser listing badly after being hammered by the Americans. "I still cringe a little thinking of how we strafed the hell out of it. Our six .50 calibers were ripping into hundreds of their sailors," he recalled.

While flying on a combat air patrol that afternoon protecting American ships in pursuit of enemy vessels attempting to leave Truk, Vraciu noted that another group of American pilots mistook the U.S.

Above: Vraciu sits on the wing of his F6F-3 Hellcat nicknamed "Gadget" shortly after combat over Truk Island in February 1944. Notice the cartoon character Felix the Cat carrying a bomb, an image used as Fighting Squadron 6's insignia.

Left: Navy pilots such as Vraciu wore a khaki cotton flying suit while in action. They also were equipped with a khaki cloth flying helmet with leather earphone covers and chin cup plus goggles.

fleet for the Japanese and had started to align their aircraft to attack them. Luckily, another pilot noticed the mistake and shouted out a warning over the radio, averting what could have been "a friendly fire disaster," said Vraciu.

Sailors and aircrews of Task Force 58 had much to be proud of during that first attack on Truk. For a loss of only four aircraft, the Americans had shot down more than thirty Japanese in the air and destroyed another forty on the ground. The enemy struck back with a vengeance, however, late in the evening on February 17. A Japanese torpedo plane, following the wake made by the *Intrepid* as it sailed along, dropped a torpedo that slammed into the flattop's starboard quarter about fifteen feet below its waterline. The resulting explosion knocked Vraciu out of his bunk, flooded several of the ship's compartments, and jammed its rudder, making it hard to steer the vessel.

Eventually, the *Intrepid* had to leave the area and return to Pearl Harbor for repairs. Strong winds, however, interfered enough with the ship's course that it ended up headed the wrong way—toward Tokyo. "Right then I wasn't interested in going in that direction," Captain Sprague later said. To help correct the situation, the crew constructed a makeshift sail that soon had them back on course. The *Intrepid* arrived safely at Pearl Harbor on February 24, 1944.

With its flattop out of commission, the members of Fighter Squadron 6 received orders to return to the United States for a needed break. Vraciu, however, wanted to remain. "I worked hard to get out there," he noted, "so I wasn't about to go back home. I had the feeling that a fighter pilot should be where the action was." Vraciu received permission from his commanding officer to go to the commander of air forces in the Pacific and obtain a transfer to another squadron still in the combat area. The officer who heard Vraciu's request thought he was crazy, but agreed to the transfer.

The evening before, Vraciu had run into Mark Bright of Anderson, Indiana, who had also achieved ace status (Bright later died on a strafing mission over Guam). The two men had attended DePauw University together and Bright suggested that Vraciu join Fighting Squadron 16, nicknamed the "Pistol Packing Airedales" for the logo emblazoned on their airplanes on the USS *Lexington*. "The suggestion was well received, and that's what I did," said Vraciu. He reported to his new leader, Lieutenant Commander Paul Buie, on February 27.

As a final farewell to his former squadron, Vraciu borrowed a Hellcat and used it to buzz the escort carrier USS *White Plains* that was taking his former shipmates from Hawaii to Alameda, California. "I'm sorry to say that I think, in the process, I disrupted the CVE's gunnery practice for a short while," he chuckled. If those pilots returning home knew the opportunities in the air that awaited Vraciu in the coming months, they might have decided to live with the danger and remain in combat as well.

5

THE TURKEY SHOOT

By the spring of 1944, American forces in the Pacific had made substantial progress in the war against Japan. Troops under the command of General Douglas MacArthur were poised to attack a string of enemy bases on New Guinea, the world's second largest island, while air, land, and sea forces under the overall direction of Admiral Chester Nimitz looked to tackle Saipan, Tinian, and Guam (a former U.S. possession) in the Mariana Islands, located about 1,300 miles southeast of Tokyo.

Taking the islands in the Marianas would disrupt Japan's supply lines to its bases in the South Pacific and limit the ability of Truk, a major enemy stronghold in the Caroline Islands, from continuing to play a major role in the war. Saipan and Tinian were also looked on with anticipation by the U.S. Army Air Corps as the perfect places on which to construct airfields for their new advanced bomber—the four-engine B-29 Superfortress, a plane with enough range to begin hitting Japanese cities.

In preparation for these operations, fast carrier task forces were dispatched to strike at Japanese airfields, removing them as a threat in the process. As a new member of Fighting Squadron 16 on the USS *Lexington*, Alex Vraciu flew a number of missions against targets at such varied locations as Mille and Palau islands, Woleai and Truk atolls, and Hollandia in western New Guinea. On three flights over Palau Island in the western Carolines, Vraciu destroyed thirteen aircraft parked alongside the runway at the island's airfield.

Other missions, however, were less fruitful. "At Hollandia . . . the Army Air Corps had already done a pretty thorough job on the fields—so much so that there were only pieces left," Vraciu noted. He also remembered missing a small Japanese boat "by an embarrassingly large margin" while experimenting with skip bombing (a low-level bombing technique used against vessels whereby a pilot lobbed his bomb at a low level like a stone on the water to hit the target). "Recognizing that my technique could use some practice," Vraciu said, "I arranged for my division to get some much-needed practice at the earliest opportunity." The extra work paid off later during the invasion of Saipan.

While opposition in the air was limited during these missions, danger always lurked in the background. While Vraciu prepared to take off on one occasion for the strikes on Palau, the crew chief responsible for maintaining the Hellcat told him that a previous pilot

had complained that something had been wrong with the plane. "I had not had a problem with a Hellcat before, so I said, 'Sure thing, chief!' or some cocky stuff," Vraciu said. He proceeded to

Admiral Chester Nimitz straps on a helmet while visiting a U.S. Navy ship, circa 1944. Upon his graduation from the U.S. Naval Academy, Nimitz had been described in the yearbook as a man "of cheerful yesterdays and confident tomorrows."

climb to an altitude of twenty-five thousand feet and started to circle around the fleet. All of a sudden, he noticed an odd smell ("like burnt green peppers") coming from the engine.

The engine problem got worse and enough smoke entered the cockpit that Vraciu had to crack open his canopy. He quickly radioed to the carrier that he needed to land, but received word to wait as they were not in a position to take him aboard. "I gave the duty carrier my hook down pass on the port side, which is the emergency signal," he said. "I remember seeing some guy with a paint brush in his hand as I was going by, and just then the engine cut out dead!" With his engine gone and no power, Vraciu had to make a water landing.

Part of the duties of destroyers in the fleet was to pick up pilots who had to ditch in the water. As a reward for returning airmen to carriers, destroyer crews often received ice cream—something the larger ships in the fleet had storage space to carry, but was a scarce item on the smaller destroyer. As Vraciu waited for rescue, he said some funny ideas crossed through his mind. "You're in the water and the first thought I had was, 'My God! It's deep down there!'" He worried about the possibility of having his fighter boots slip off his feet and sink to the bottom. "The toggles on my Mae West [life jacket] were jammed, so I was treading water for a long time until they [the destroyer crew] threw me a life preserver," Vraciu added.

The navy pilot had some time to think about his predicament as the destroyer had to make three passes before it could pick him up. Vraciu finally yelled up to the crew: "What's the matter! Don't you want the ice cream?" Eventually, sailors hauled the thoroughly soaked pilot aboard and, using a technique called high lining (a basketlike device attached to lines between ships at sea), transferred Vraciu back to the *Lexington*. "I found the destroyer people are just great. They can't be any nicer. Maybe it's because they're going to get ice cream for you later on," he laughed.

On April 29, 1944, Vraciu gained his first aerial victories as a member of Fighting Squadron 16. The kills came during another raid on the Japanese airbase at Truk. The base had recently received approximately a hundred planes from the airfield at Rabaul on New Britain. While escorting bombers after hitting Truk on a morning mission, Vraciu and the rest of his flight were jumped by a small group of enemy Zeros. "We simply pounced on them and destroyed them at *their* best performance altitude—down low," he said. "It was a no-contest affair after we had them boxed in."

Operating at low altitudes posed more dangers than just opposition from the enemy. For one of his two kills, Vraciu attacked a Zero whose pilot attempted a loop maneuver at a "ridiculously low altitude just at the time that I got in a good burst. It seemed to stop him dead, and he went into the water smoking." Unfortunately, a fellow Hellcat pilot during the same fight tried to follow a Zero in a loop at low altitude; both crashed into the sea.

Vraciu participated in another escort mission that afternoon. This time his luck almost ran out. While flying at nine thousand feet and making preparations to strafe one of the runways on Truk, Vraciu's Hellcat came under fierce antiaircraft fire. "Part of the flak passed through my cockpit just in front of my face, showering the cockpit with Plexiglass," he said. "My hydraulic system was riddled, and the landing gear dropped down part way."

His wingman protected him as Vraciu flew back to the fleet. Because his landing gear could not be locked in place for a safe landing on the deck of the *Lexington*, he was given the choice of either parachuting over the fleet or ditching into the water. Vraciu decided to remain with his plane and risk putting it down in the sea. Since his first experience at ditching, he had learned to first lower the Hellcat's tailhook in order to "feel the wave" before landing, and for this attempt his engine still worked. "Even though the waves were kind of heavy," Vraciu noted, "I landed on the backside of the wave rather than hitting it head on." (Those pilots who hit waves head on often found their planes were ripped apart in the process.)

Vraciu had to remain on the destroyer overnight due to rough seas. The crew treated him very well. The captain gave him his sea cabin and Vraciu's flight clothes were taken away, cleaned, dried, and returned to him in about thirty minutes. Vraciu also had the opportunity to stay on the bridge to see how the ship operated. Having served only on larger aircraft carriers, however, the Hoosier pilot was unfamiliar with just how uncomfortable a ride could be on a destroyer when the waves were pitching the smaller ship about.

Feeling some discomfort in his left eye that night, Vraciu discovered that some of the Plexiglass from the shattered canopy of his Hellcat had embedded itself in his eye. "The ship's doctor deadened the eyeball and scraped out the offending glass," Vraciu said. The pilot earned another keepsake from his second ditching within a five-week period—a reputation from the flagship staff as "Grumman's Best Customer."

The next morning, when transfer back to his carrier did not seem imminent, Vraciu asked the destroyer's captain if he could send a message to W. J. "Gus" Widhelm, the officer in charge of air operations for Admiral Marc Mitscher on the *Lexington*. The captain agreed and Vraciu, with the same prankish nature he displayed while a college student, sent the following communication: "Gus, get me off this danged roller coaster, or I'll vote for MacArthur, so help me!" The general had received consideration as a possible presidential candidate back in the United States, but was unpopular with those serving in the navy in the Pacific because he had referred to ships assigned to him as "my navy." Vraciu noted that he figured, "If that doesn't get me off, I'll have to ride this destroyer all the way back to Ulithi [an atoll in the Carolines that served as a major navy base in the war] before returning to my carrier."

Widhelm, described by Vraciu as a "real character" and an officer the crew could joke with, let his wayward pilot stew for a while before responding. "I said to the captain of the destroyer, 'What do you think? Do you think I'm dead on this one?' He said, 'No. Let's wait awhile,'" recalled Vraciu. Finally, the destroyer received a message from Widhelm that read: "Captain, in order to conserve aircraft, desire you retain my 'birdman' until we reach Ulithi, at which time we will transport him back via rubber boat." Fortunately for Vraciu, Widhelm was joking; about forty-five minutes later, the *Lexington* signaled the destroyer to come alongside to transfer over its wayward pilot.

When he got back to the carrier, Vraciu met a grinning Widhelm who immediately took him up to the *Lexington*'s bridge for a meeting with Mitscher. Once there, Widhelm said: "Admiral, here's the character that sent that message." It marked the first time Vraciu had been introduced to Mitscher, but it would not be the last time the two men communicated with one another.

The operations in support of MacArthur by Vraciu and Fighting Squadron 16 that spring were just the preliminaries to one of the major engagements of the war in the Pacific—the Battle of the Philippine Sea. The battle grew out of Operation Forager, the American plan to capture Saipan, Tinian, and Guam. Saipan was the first target, with the island to be invaded on June 15, 1944, by more than eight thousand troops

A Hellcat lands aboard the USS *Lexington* during the Great Marianas Turkey Shoot phase of the Battle of the Philippine Sea, June 19, 1944. On guard against a possible Japanese attack, sailors man the 40mm guns in the foreground and the 20mm guns along the starboard side of the flight deck.

from the Second and Fourth Marine divisions, with the army's Twenty-seventh Division in reserve. Mitscher's Task Force 58, part of the U.S. Fifth Fleet under the command of Admiral Raymond Spruance, helped to protect the landings with its fifteen aircraft carriers carrying nine hundred planes, as well as a number of new, modern battleships.

All of this activity was sure to draw the attention of the Japanese, who were surprised, however, that the U.S. attack came in the Marianas, as they were expecting an engagement in either the Palaus or the Carolines. Nevertheless, Japan's First Mobile Fleet, commanded by Admiral Jisaburo Ozawa, set sail to tackle the Americans with five large carriers, four light flattops, five battleships, and assorted cruisers, destroyers, and oilers for refueling. Ozawa and his officers hoped to wage "a decisive battle" that would turn the tide of the war to Japan's favor.

Because they lacked armor plating and self-sealing fuel tanks, Japanese planes were lighter than their American counterparts and could fly greater distances. Ozawa hoped to use this advantage, catch sight of the enemy fleet first, and attack before the Americans knew what had hit them. The admiral knew he would be outnumbered in carrier strength by his opponent, but counted on assistance from five hundred land-based aircraft on Japanese bases in the area. Ozawa also hoped planes from his carriers could rearm and refuel after attacks by landing on Guam's airfields. They could then take off and strike the U.S. ships again on the way back to their carriers. Most of these enemy aircraft and airfields, however, had been devastated by U.S. raids leading up to the Saipan invasion.

A number of the pilots expected to carry out Ozawa's orders, however, were no longer the veterans who had run wild throughout the Pacific early in the war. The Japanese who were to tangle with the

Americans had limited experience in the air, with most receiving only two to six months of training, compared to approximately two years worth for their opponents. These fliers were unsure in battle and did not know the proper method for attacking ships at sea.

Vraciu and the rest of his squadron were kept busy attacking targets on Saipan leading up to the invasion. Escorting a group of SBD Dauntless dive-bombers north of the island, Vraciu, thanks to his good vision, spotted a reconnaissance Japanese G4M Mitsubishi Betty bomber at an altitude of eighteen thousand feet. After receiving permission from the leader of the bombers to go after the bogey, he dropped his belly tank with extra fuel and cranked his engine to full power to close the gap between the two planes. "I climbed up in his blind spot, directly underneath it, at a sharp angle," Vraciu recalled. As he reached the Betty's altitude, someone in the seven-man crew saw the Hellcat approaching and warned the pilot. "The Betty quickly lowered its nose and started diving to build up speed," said Vraciu. "So I made one pass and burned him." The victory boosted Vraciu's total to twelve.

The quick victory caused some dissension among the other Americans fighters who had hoped to down the enemy bomber themselves, as the Betty was known throughout the fleet for being easy to catch on fire (American pilots nicknamed it "the flying Zippo [lighter]" and "flying cigar"). One frustrated Hellcat pilot yelled, "Vraciu, you S.O.B.," over the radio for all to hear. "I ran into him stateside once while we were home on leave, and he reminded me about the occasion," Vraciu said. "He was still unhappy about it."

Other missions also proved to be eventful over Saipan. Vraciu's earlier decision to perfect his skip-bombing technique paid off when he was able to place a five-hundred-pound bomb into the waterline of a large cargo vessel, sending it to the bottom of the harbor. On another mission, however, Japanese defenders on the island showed they were still able to hit back at the Americans, and the Hellcat proved it could take an enormous amount of punishment and keep flying. Vraciu had agreed to fly for another pilot unable to make his flight. While strafing a seaplane ramp on Saipan, his plane caught some flak in its engine. Although his oil pressure was dropping much too fast for comfort, Vraciu managed to bring his damaged aircraft safely back to his carrier. After he climbed out of his Hellcat, Vraciu made sure to find the officer he had replaced on the mission and told him, "From now on, no more taking hops for you."

Officers serving with Task Force 58 were all anticipating a showdown with the Japanese fleet. A confidant Widhelm came down to the pilot's ready room on the *Lexington* during the Saipan operation and bet the fighter squadron a thousand dollars that they would have a fleet engagement within seven days. Vraciu had been on a combat air patrol at the time of Widhelm's challenge, and when he returned only $125 was left of the thousand-dollar bet, as the other pilots had already placed their wagers. Vraciu agreed to risk $125 and waited to see what would happen next.

On the afternoon of June 18, search planes from Ozawa's First Mobile Fleet located the American ships. Because of the lateness of the sighting, however, Ozawa's main attack did not occur until the morning of the next day. Hoping to inspire his sailors, the admiral sent out a message repeating the orders that Admiral Heihachiro Togo had sent before his navy crushed the Russian fleet at the crucial Battle of Tsushima Strait in 1905: "The fate of the Empire rests on this one battle. Every man is expected to do his utmost."

A Japanese torpedo plane is aflame after a failed attack on the escort carrier USS *Kitkun Bay* during the invasion of Saipan in June 1944.

Aviators in the American fleet were anxiously awaiting a showdown with the Japanese, believing they had a chance to deliver a stunning blow to the enemy flattops. Their commander Spruance, however, moved cautiously to counter the enemy. His first priority was to protect the landing operation on Saipan. Spruance feared that if he went pell-mell after the Japanese, the enemy would divide its forces and make an "end run" to attack the vulnerable transport and supply ships. A worried Spruance asked the officers in charge of the Saipan invasion if he might move the vessels away from the area, but they pointed out that troops on the island would need the food and ammunition stored on the ships if they were to succeed. "Well, get everything that you don't absolutely need out of here to the eastward," Spruance said, "and I will join up with Mitscher and Task Force 58 and try to keep the Japs off your neck."

Early in the morning on June 19, Ozawa launched the first of four waves of attackers against the carriers of Mitscher's task force. The American admiral stood ready; he positioned a circle of battleships under Vice Admiral Willis Lee to protect the carrier groups with their heavy antiaircraft fire. Fighter director officers on the carriers received intelligence on the position and movement of the enemy's aircraft through intercepts made by Lieutenant Charles Sims, who spoke Japanese. These reports were relayed to the circling Hellcats in the combat air patrol. American dive-bombers and torpedo planes were shunted aside for the time being on carrier decks, or sent away from the action so they would not be shot at by their own forces.

Vraciu and Fighting Squadron 16 were on alert on the deck of the *Lexington* to backup the combat air patrol already in the air. At approximately ten o'clock a group of twelve Hellcats—three divisions of four planes each—were launched from the flattop. Over his radio,

Vraciu heard an FDO indicate that the planes should take a heading of 250 degrees and climb to twenty-five thousand feet at full power. "Overhead, converging contrails of fighters from other carriers could be seen heading in the same direction," Vraciu remembered.

The squadron's leader, Lieutenant Commander Paul Buie, who flew a plane with a new engine, started to pull away from the other Hellcats. Vraciu experienced problems with his engine, as it threw a film of oil on his windshield, making it hard for him to see. His engine's problems also limited his altitude to just twenty thousand feet. As the Hellcats climbed, Vraciu's wingman, Ensign Homer Brockmeyer, repeatedly pointed toward his leader's wings (he had to use hand signals because the flight was observing radio silence). Vraciu thought Brockmeyer had seen the enemy, but what Vraciu did not know was that his wings were not securely locked into place—a situation that "explained Brock's frantic pointing." (The Hellcats' wings could be folded for easier storage below deck on a carrier.)

Vraciu's group received orders to return to the task force and orbit overhead at twenty thousand feet. "We had barely returned when the FDO vectored us on a heading of 265 degrees," he said. "Something in his voice told us that he had a good one on the string. The bogeys were seventy-five miles away when reported, and we headed outbound in hope of meeting them halfway. I saw two other groups of Hellcats converging off to starboard, four in one group and three in another."

About twenty-five miles from the fleet, Vraciu saw three enemy aircraft and closed in on them. Believing there must be more Japanese in the area, he used his excellent eyesight to pick out a large mass of at least fifty airplanes about two thousand feet below him, streaking toward the U.S. ships. "I remember thinking that this could develop into that once-in-a-lifetime fighter pilot's dream," Vraciu recalled.

Vraciu waves to the camera from the F6F-3 Hellcat he flew into combat during the Battle of the Philippine Sea. During the action, fifteen Hellcat squadrons shot down 371 enemy plans, while losing only fourteen pilots.

The enemy formation, which included a number of Yokosuka D4Y Judy dive-bombers with their two-man crews, did not have any Zero fighter escorts. Diving in for an attack, Vraciu noted out of the corner of his eye that another Hellcat had begun his run on the same Judy he had targeted for destruction. "He was too close for comfort and seemed not to see me, so I aborted my run," he said. "There were enough cookies on the plate for everyone, I thought." Flying under the formation, Vraciu got a good look at the enemy and radioed back to the U.S. fleet the composition of the attacking planes.

Pulling his Hellcat up and over the formation, Vraciu picked out another Judy to attack. "It was wildly maneuvering, and the Japanese rear gunner was squirting away as I came down from behind," he noted. "I worked in close, gave him a burst and set him afire quickly. The Judy headed for the water, trailing a long plume of smoke." Vraciu pulled up again and came in behind two other Judys, turning both into flaming wrecks. "The sky appeared full of smoke and pieces of aircraft as we tried to ride herd on the remaining enemy planes in an effort to keep them from scattering," he added.

The enemy flew closer and closer to the American fleet despite the withering fire from the attacking Hellcats. Because the oil on his windshield restricted his vision, Vraciu worked in close to his next victim so he could get a clear shot. "I gave him a short burst, but it was enough," he said. "The rounds went right into the sweet spot at the root of his wing. Other rounds must have hit the pilot or control cables, as the burning plane twisted crazily out of control."

Vraciu headed next for a group of three Judys preparing to peel off for their bombing runs close to a group of American battleships. As the first Judy began its dive, Vraciu noticed a black puff of smoke appear next to him, the result of antiaircraft fire from five-inch guns below.

Above: While back on board the USS *Lexington*, a grinning Vraciu holds up six fingers to signify his tallies of Japanese aircraft on June 19, 1944. **Left:** Admiral Marc Mitscher congratulates Vraciu for his skillful flying as part of the Great Marianas Turkey Shoot.

Disregarding the flak, Vraciu overtook the nearest bomber. "It seemed that I had scarcely touched the gun trigger when his engine began to come to pieces," he recalled. "The Judy started smoking then began torching alternately on and off as it disappeared below me." Another short burst at the other Judy "produced astonishing results," said Vraciu. The plane disintegrated in a tremendous explosion that made Vraciu yank his plane about wildly to avoid hitting any pieces. "I must have hit his bomb, I guess," he reasoned. "I had seen planes explode before, but *never* like this!"

With another Japanese destroyed, Vraciu radioed to the fleet: "Splash number six. There's one more ahead and he's diving on a BB [battleship]. But I don't think he'll make it." The words had barely left his mouth when the remaining Judy caught a direct hit and blew up. "He had run into a solid curtain of steel from the battlewagon," Vraciu noted.

Catching his breath, Vraciu looked around the sky and could see only American planes still flying. Looking back over the route his squadron had taken, he saw Hellcats and "a thirty-five-mile long pattern of flaming oil slicks." In a matter of just eight minutes, Vraciu had downed six Japanese aircraft—a result that gave him a great deal of satisfaction. "I felt that I had contributed my personal payback for Pearl Harbor," he said. This good feeling began to evaporate, however, when some "trigger-happy gun crews" from the American fleet mistook him for the enemy and started firing at him. He uttered a few choice words over the radio and was able to land his Hellcat with no further problems.

As he taxied up the deck of the carrier, Vraciu flashed six fingers to the bridge. The pilot repeated the gesture after exiting his Hellcat—a moment captured on film as he signed the yellow maintenance sheet at the tail of his aircraft. Although Admiral Mitscher was careful to stay out of the photographs being taken then, several days after the battle he noted: "I'd like to pose with him [Vraciu]. Not for publication. To keep for myself." (Vraciu later named his youngest son, Marc, in honor of Mitscher.)

The crew that maintained the Hellcats discovered that Vraciu had used only 360 rounds of the 2,400 available in his fully armed aircraft to shoot down the six enemy planes. "As can be expected, there was a great deal of excitement later in the ready room—including the liberal use of hands to punctuate the aerial victories," Vraciu remembered.

Other American squadrons enjoyed just as good a day's shooting as had Vraciu and Fighting Squadron 16. During the four attacks made against Task Force 58, the Japanese had used 373 planes—only 100 survived to return to their carriers. Hellcats also shot down an additional 50 land-based enemy aircraft. The Americans lost only 29 planes in this lopsided affair. According to Vraciu, a junior lieutenant from his squadron, Ziggy Neff, had the perfect comment to make at the end of the day's fighting. "He apparently came from a hunting background and just happened to use that hunting jargon phrase in his postflight briefing, saying, 'It was just like a turkey shoot!'" said Vraciu. The phrase stuck, and the battle became known as the Great Marianas Turkey Shoot.

Some Japanese planes had made it through the gauntlet of Hellcats and antiaircraft fire. They only managed to slightly damage the battleship USS *South Dakota* and the carrier USS *Bunker Hill*. Although the American fleet had not been able to engage the enemy, U.S. submarines were able to slip through and deliver lethal blows. Torpedoes from the USS *Albacore* hit the Japanese carrier *Taiho*, Ozawa's flagship. Although the damage had been contained, a rookie officer had let dangerous gases circulate throughout the ship's ventilation system—the deadly mixture exploded and sank the carrier, killing 1,650 sailors. Another American submarine, the USS *Cavalla*, hit the carrier *Shokaku*, a veteran of Pearl Harbor, with four torpedoes that caused fires to rage out of control. The carrier sank with a loss of 1,263 men.

Widhelm had not forgotten about the thousand-dollar bet he had made with the pilots on the *Lexington*. The airmen, however, as they downed cup after cup of hot coffee, were not yet ready to part with their money. They pointed out to the officer that "a fleet engagement

The USS *Bunker Hill* narrowly escapes a Japanese bomb during air attacks on June 19, 1944. The enemy plane, with its tail shot off, is about to crash into the sea, at left.

meant that we had to hit them, also, and we hadn't found them yet," Vraciu observed. "They were still out of range of our search planes." That changed late in the day on June 20. At about four in the afternoon a plane from the USS *Enterprise* finally discovered the whereabouts of Ozawa's fleet.

With daylight failing, time was short on a decision on whether or not to launch an attack against the Japanese. Mitscher consulted Widhelm, who noted: "It's going to be tight." Because of the distance involved between the two armadas (approximately three hundred miles), there existed a good chance that many of the U.S. planes would not have enough fuel to make it back to their carriers, and those who did would not be able to make it back until night had fallen. Despite the risks, orders were sent to launch aircraft, and a force of seventy-seven dive-bombers, fifty-four torpedo planes, and eighty-five fighters responded. The pilots had one main task in mind: "Get the carriers."

Pilots on the *Lexington* were in and out of their ready rooms all day expecting a strike against the Japanese. When Vraciu finally received word of the enemy's sighting, he said he and the rest of the fighter pilots figured their Hellcats would have enough fuel for the mission, but the same could not be said for the bombers. Many were also worried about the possibility of trying to land their planes at night. Vraciu did have two months worth of training in night operations from his previous service with Fighting Squadron 6.

Vraciu and eight other Hellcats flew escort for a group of fifteen dive-bombers and six torpedo planes. "I saluted to the bridge as I took off," he said, "because I didn't think I was coming back. A lot of us didn't." The faster fighters had to continuously weave back and forth because of the bombers' slower cruising speed. The group came under immediate attack by a horde of Zeroes when it reached its target. A

The Japanese aircraft carrier *Zuikaku* (center) and two destroyers frantically attempt to avoid attacks by U.S. carrier aircraft during the Battle of the Philippine Sea on June 20, 1944. Although struck by several bombs, *Zuikaku* survived.

huge cumulus cloud hampered operations, as it separated Hellcats flying top cover from the planes below. "Brock and I were the only planes remaining with the bombers at that time and we appeared surrounded," Vraciu remembered. Glancing down, he saw that one of the Avenger torpedo planes had been hit by the enemy and had caught on fire. The crew bailed out successfully and was later rescued.

The Japanese pilots encountered by Vraciu and his wingmen were tough opponents. "Now these guys were *good*," said Vraciu. Both sides battled for position, hoping to slip in and rake their opponent with machine-gun and/or cannon fire. Outnumbered, Vraciu and Brockmeyer went into the defensive "Thach Weave" to hold off the Japanese and perhaps get into position to shoot down the enemy.

As the Americans struggled to survive, one of the enemy fighters caught on to Brockmeyer's tail and fired. Vraciu was able to shoot down the Zero that had hit his wingman, but he had "the sad experience of seeing Brock going down. I still think I hear him faintly say, 'I'm hit.' I was able to get in another good burst at one of them, but I couldn't tell whether he went down. I damaged it, I'm sure."

Surrounded, Vraciu used a last-ditch defensive maneuver, diving down and away from the enemy. He flew on to the rendezvous area where he joined up with a damaged Avenger from another U.S. carrier. The pilot of the torpedo plane signaled to Vraciu that he was low on gas and did not have enough for a return to the American fleet. "The sun had already started to disappear on the horizon," Vraciu said. "He stayed right down low and didn't climb up for altitude." Eventually, the Avenger joined a group of seven planes circling low on the water; all of them were low on fuel and intended on ditching in the water. "It was dark by that time, and I gave them all a heartfelt salute," said Vraciu. "I don't know what ever happened to all those guys."

Still several hundred miles away from the *Lexington*, Vraciu found himself alone in the darkening sky. Thanks to the lessons he had learned from Butch O'Hare, he had been able to conserve his fuel and had enough to return home. Vraciu climbed his Hellcat to eight thousand feet to improve his radio reception so he could latch onto the directional signal from the fleet to help guide him back. Other American pilots were not as fortunate as Vraciu. "Some of the guys were real cool coming back that night," he recalled, "but some of them were breaking down—sobbing—on the air. It was a dark and black ocean out there. I could empathize with them, but it got so bad that I had to turn my radio off for a while."

Back on Task Force 58, officers were worried about their returning airmen. To aid in their return, the fleet sent out a signal for the pilots to land on the nearest carrier they could find. Mitscher also sent out a simple order to his carriers: "Turn on the lights." Otto Romanelli, who served on the *Lexington*, noted that he and other crew members "felt the tightness in our throats relax. We were doing the only thing that could be done to lead our 'kid brothers' home, at the risk of exposing our ships to any [enemy] submarines or bombers in the area." The pilots who had been left behind on the carriers were astonished by Mitscher's order. "They stood open mouthed for the sheer audacity of asking the Japs to come and get us," noted Lieutenant Commander Robert Winston. "Then a spontaneous cheer went up. To hell with the Japs around us. Our pilots were not to be expendable."

Some of the American flattops went as far as to point their twenty-four-inch searchlights straight up into the air to act as a beacon for their wayward pilots, and destroyers and cruisers helped by shooting illuminating star shells into the sky. One pilot described the scene as "a Hollywood premiere, Chinese New Year, and the Fourth of July all rolled into one." In the confusion, some pilots mistook destroyers for carriers, tried to land on them, and crashed or had to ditch into the sea. (Luckily for the U.S. fleet, there were no Japanese submarines in the area to take advantage of the situation.)

The sudden burst of lights from the fleet, however, stunned Vraciu and led him to think he had taken a wrong turn and ended up at Yap Island, a Japanese base in the Carolines. He also thought about "all these revolting things the bomber pilots used to say, that fighter pilots couldn't navigate. I thought, 'Well, it's coming home to roost now.'"

Although advised to land at the nearest carrier, Vraciu had enough fuel so he could wait and try to get back on the *Lexington*. He wanted to sleep in his own bunk that night and was "dehydrated and thirsty as hell, and kept thinking about the 'scuttlebutt' [water fountain] on the ship." Approaching his ship, he discovered a real mess. "Planes were everywhere, every ship was lit up, and some carriers had lost position," he said. "They had overlapping traffic patterns; the upwind leg of some carriers seemed to merge with the downwind leg of others. I don't know why there weren't any collisions [between the vessels]."

After circling overhead for a while, the way home began to clear and Vraciu started his approach to his ship. As he tried to land, however, the landing signal officer had a constant "wave off." A damaged plane very low on fuel from another carrier had ignored a wave off from the LSO and crashed while trying to set down on the *Lexington*, killing and wounding some of the crew. Vraciu turned away and landed next door on the *Enterprise* on his first pass.

As he taxied his plane forward, Vraciu heard the blare of the crash horn, signaling that the aircraft landing behind him had slammed into the deck. "I was urged, after parking my plane, to get off the flight deck as quickly as possible," he noted. "So I got off the flight deck in a hurry!" Vraciu retired to one of the ship's ready rooms and found that the only other pilot he recognized was a dive-bomber from the *Lexington.* "Thoughtfully," Vraciu said, "the ship provided us with medicinal brandy to relax us." He later discovered that each of the seven survivors from his squadron had landed on a different carrier that night. "It was a sobering thing—probably one of the toughest flights

Lieutenant Ronald "Rip" Gift relaxes with other pilots in a ready room on board the carrier USS *Monterey* after landing on the flattop at night following strikes on the Japanese fleet on June 20, 1944. Note the encouragement to pilots to "Get the Carriers" on the chalkboard in the background.

that any of the guys involved had ever had because of the way it turned out," Vraciu added.

Getting back to their own carriers after the battle proved to be a deadly task for some members of Vraciu's squadron. The pilots that had landed on different carriers were supposed to fly a combat air patrol the next morning, at the conclusion of which they were to return to their own ships. "Well, they barely got us airborne—they had put belly tanks on us again—and they said, 'Return to your respective carriers now!'" said Vraciu. As he prepared to land back on the *Lexington*, Vraciu saw the pilot ahead of him, a young ensign named Seyfferle, spin in while landing because of the extra weight of his full belly tank and crash into the sea. "I retracted my wheels and took a pass at the accident scene because it occurred right in front of me, and I told the carrier, 'He's gone!'" Vraciu remembered.

What came to be known as the "Mission beyond Darkness" led to the loss of eighty of the 216 American planes launched against the Japanese fleet, with the majority of the aircraft lost not through enemy action, but due to lack of fuel or accidents. Rescue efforts for lost crewmen were successful; only sixteen pilots and thirty-three crewmen died. The June 20 strike did inflict considerable damage on the Japanese. U.S. planes sank the light carrier *Hiyo* and damaged two others. In addition, several tankers were destroyed and a battleship and cruiser received several hits, putting them out of action for a time. Also, sixty-five enemy planes were downed during the attack, leaving Ozawa with just thirty-five surviving aircraft from the 430 he had under his command the day before.

The Battle of the Philippine Sea left many American naval officers upset. They believed the U.S. Navy had held in its hand a chance to destroy the Japanese fleet, but Spruance had been too cautious in going after the enemy. "It was the chance of a century missed," complained Read Admiral Joseph "Jocko" Clark. There were others, however, including Fleet Admiral Ernest King, commander in chief of naval operations during the war, who believed that Spruance had made the right decision to pursue his primary mission of protecting the operation on Saipan. Although Spruance insisted that the navy had accomplished its mission, he did note years after the battle: "It was disappointing that we did not do more. Midway was much more satisfying."

With his nineteenth victory on June 20, Vraciu became the navy's leading ace in the Pacific—a figure that stood up over the next four months. After participating in missions against the airfield on Guam to soften it up for the coming invasion by American forces, Vraciu and the rest of Fighting Squadron 16 were taken out of combat. They rode the *Enterprise* back to Pearl Harbor and from there sailed on the escort carrier USS *Makin Island* to San Diego, California, and were rewarded by the navy with thirty days of leave. Vraciu soon discovered that his exploits in the air over the Philippine Sea had made him a hero to those on the home front.

6

THE RELUCTANT HERO

On the afternoon of August 6, 1944, residents of the twin cities of Indiana Harbor and East Chicago in northwest Indiana, weary of food and gasoline rationing and tired from fashioning the weapons needed for victory, gathered to honor one of their own for his achievements on the battlefield. Flanked by his high school principal and a fellow naval officer, the pilot, dressed in his dazzling white dress uniform, acknowledged the cheers of the crowd as he rode in the back of an open convertible through the city streets. Alex Vraciu had come home.

Promoted to the rank of full lieutenant upon his arrival in San Diego, California, Vraciu had returned as the leading navy ace in the Pacific. The navy saw in Vraciu's status as one of its leading pilots an opportunity to promote the service and its accomplishments in the Pacific theater to the American public. Navy officials asked Vraciu to fly a captured Japanese Mitsubishi Zero on a nationwide tour and offered the possibility of having him and another pilot fly a Grumman Hellcat and SBD Dauntless dive-bomber to various cities to promote the sale of war bonds to help fund the conflict. These possibilities were hanging over Vraciu's head, but first he tried to enjoy his leave time.

Vraciu arrived home earlier than expected. To give city officials time to plan his celebration, he spent a week at the Chicago home of his uncle, John Tincu, who a year earlier had promised his nephew a hundred dollars for every Japanese plane he shot down. On hand to greet Vraciu at the Chicago airport on his arrival were his parents and sister, East Chicago mayor Frank Migas, Chief of Police Walter D. Conroy, and commander of Twin City American Legion Post 266 A. W. Sirlin. While Vraciu told reporters he longed for the taste of strawberry shortcake, his uncle expressed relief that his nephew made it home when he did. "If Alex had stayed [in the Pacific] any longer," said Tincu, "I'd had to buy the whole Jap air force."

The impending celebration seemed a bit much for Vraciu, who told Migas that if he had his way, he would rather return home without any fuss. Despite his protests, Vraciu, on August 6, received a welcome described by a local newspaper as "one of the greatest demonstrations in the industrial city's history." Riding in an open convertible with his former principal, Russell F. Robinson, and a navy official, Commander Lewis Lee, Vraciu waved to the crowds that lined city streets as he made

EAST CHICAGO PUBLIC LIBRARY

Flanked by Commander Lewis Lee (left) and Russell Robinson, former principal at Washington High School in East Chicago, Indiana, Vraciu rides in the back of a convertible on his way to a celebration in his honor at Block Stadium.

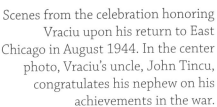

Scenes from the celebration honoring Vraciu upon his return to East Chicago in August 1944. In the center photo, Vraciu's uncle, John Tincu, congratulates his nephew on his achievements in the war.

his way to a ceremony in his honor at Block Stadium. A motorcycle escort and nearly fifty cars followed Vraciu as he made his way through the community.

At the stadium, a crowd estimated at anywhere from five thousand to six thousand in size was on hand for the 2 p.m. program. As Vraciu arrived at the arena, he was greeted by an honor guard from the American Legion and music from the Lake County Ladies Drum and Bugle Corps. During the three-hour ceremony, Indiana governor Henry Schricker praised Vraciu for adding "a glorious page to Indiana's history. He represents 300,000 Indiana men in the armed forces and his heroic service reminds those at home that they have a duty to perform,

Photographs of Kathryn Horn at home in East Chicago during World War II (left) and as a sophomore student at Indiana University in Bloomington (right). Vraciu and Horn were married on August 24, 1944.

a duty without which Lieutenant Vraciu and his comrades would be unable to succeed."

To honor his victories in the air, the East Chicago community presented Vraciu with fifteen hundred dollars worth of war bonds. His uncle also made good on his promise, giving his nephew an additional twenty-five hundred dollars in government bonds for shooting down nineteen Japanese aircraft. (Vraciu had to cash in the bonds and use the money to help pay for his expenses during his subsequent travels across the country for war-bond rallies and other appearances.) "How could I know that out of hundreds of thousands of boys," said Tincu, "my nephew would bag 19 enemy planes? It's a good thing for me the navy doesn't count those on the ground!" For his part, Vraciu kept his remarks short, praising residents "for the job you are doing in keeping the home front in tune with the victory march."

After the ceremony, the twenty-five-year-old Vraciu signed autographs and offered hugs and kisses to starstruck girls along the parade route. Along the way the motorcade passed by the home of one of Vraciu's former neighbors, John Horn, the late owner of the Washington Lumber Company. Vraciu ordered the car to stop and jumped out of the convertible next to a young Margaret Horn. "You don't want me," she told Vraciu, "you want my sister." She pointed to her sister, Kathryn, a senior at Indiana University, who stood on the front porch and had not gone to the ceremony. "So I walked up to her," Vraciu recalled, "and we were married in two-and-a-half weeks. Talk about a storybook deal."

The couple married on August 24 in a ceremony at Saint Patrick Catholic Church in East Chicago. They had a brief honeymoon in New York before Vraciu had to report to Jacksonville, Florida, to await further orders. At first, the navy wanted him to make additional

Above: The aircraft carrier *USS Bunker Hill* burns after a Japanese kamikaze attack near Okinawa, May 11, 1945.
Right: General Douglas MacArthur wades ashore during initial landings at Leyte in the Philippines, October 1944.

speeches around the country, but a friendly admiral used his influence to ensure that Vraciu could have his wish and return to combat.

Fighter pilots were badly needed in the Pacific at this time, as the enemy had begun kamikaze ("divine wind") attacks on American ships. Using planes filled with explosives and bombs, Japanese pilots committed suicide by crashing their aircraft into U.S. vessels, especially aircraft carriers. Admiral Chester Nimitz, commander of American naval forces in the Pacific, remarked that nothing "that had happened during the war was a surprise, absolutely nothing except the kamikaze tactics toward the end; we had not visualized these."

To meet this new threat, the navy had begun to increase the size of fighter squadrons on its flattops and decrease the number of torpedo planes and dive-bombers. "Bombs and rockets were hung on the F6F [Hellcat] to make up for the bomber aircraft deletion," said Vraciu. After he arrived at Pearl Harbor, Vraciu received orders to report to Fighting Squadron 19 onboard the USS *Lexington*, which had been damaged by a kamikaze while engaged in protecting American troops landing on Leyte Island in the Philippines. "I hitched rides all over the Pacific," said Vraciu. "I ran into pilot friends that had been in some places for six months, waiting for a destroyer ride, so I wouldn't check in anywhere. I'd go to the airfield and wait to hitch a plane that was headed in my direction."

Vraciu finally made it to his assignment thanks to the help from a marine cargo pilot passing through the area. The two men had played football together at DePauw University. The pilot made room for the navy officer by leaving behind a couple of sacks of mail. Unfortunately, the squadron Vraciu was supposed to report for duty to had recently received orders to return home. The *Lexington*'s captain, Ernie Litch, took pity on the stranded pilot and transferred Vraciu to Fighting

Squadron 20, which was just transferring to the ship after service on the carrier *Enterprise*.

On December 14, 1944, Vraciu flew two missions with Fighting Squadron 20 near a former American airbase, Clark Field, in central Luzon in the northern Philippines about sixty miles from the capital of Manila. With no Japanese planes in the air, Vraciu and his fellow pilots concentrated on destroying enemy aircraft on the ground. While pulling away from a low strafing run on his afternoon mission, Vraciu realized that his plane had been hit by enemy fire in its engine's oil tank. "I knew that I'd had it," he remembered. "Oil was gushing out and going all over my canopy, and my oil pressure was rapidly dropping. There was no way I'd be able to get back to my carrier."

Pilots on the *Lexington* had been warned by the ship's intelligence officers that if they were hit and had to bail out of their aircraft over Luzon to head westward away from the lowlands, an area that held the majority of Japanese troops in the Philippines. The hilly western section of the island, which included Mount Pinatubo, an active volcano, included dense forests from which a number of guerrilla forces fighting the enemy and gathering intelligence were active. Also, it was possible for downed pilots to make their way to the coast for possible rescue by an American submarine. "It's hard to head away from the direction of your carrier," said Vraciu, "but it had to be!"

Following the fall of the Philippines to the Japanese earlier in the war, some of the American and Filipino troops had escaped and fled to the jungle or hills to continue to fight the enemy, particularly in Luzon, as U.S. Army Forces in the Far East guerrilla groups. According to historian William Manchester, by the end of 1944 more than a hundred and eighty thousand Filipinos had fought with or aided the guerrillas in some manner. These groups included former members of the Philippine army, sometimes led by American soldiers that had escaped the Bataan Death March, and the Hukbalahap (Huks), the military arm of the Communist Party of the Philippines.

Preparing to bail out of his stricken aircraft, Vraciu opened his canopy and began throwing out any items he did not want to have with him if he happened to be captured by the Japanese (any information that might be useful to the enemy). "When I dared not wait any longer, I climbed out on the wing of my plane and impulsively held on to the side of the cockpit and trailing edge of the wing—waiting—so I could get farther out of the lowlands and into the hills," he noted. "It probably was just for a matter of a few seconds, but it sure seemed like a long time."

Jumping free of the plane, Vraciu had only a short time to think before he hit the ground. "I remember coming down, saying to myself, 'Alex, what have you got yourself into this time!'" He landed about a half a kilometer away from the city of Capas in the Tarlac province. A member of the Filipino guerrilla force who lived in Capas remembered hearing Japanese antiaircraft guns "barking furiously" as he cultivated his garden. Looking up, the resistance fighter saw a lone American aircraft flying over the city to the west and Japanese soldiers gathering to follow to see if the pilot would survive the crash.

Vraciu had made up his mind that he would not allow himself to be captured by the enemy, and snatched his .45-caliber gun from his holster when he noticed about eight men running toward where he had landed. A slightly dazed Vraciu heard the group shout: "Filipino! Filipino! No shoot!" In a short time, the men had changed the pilot's oil-soaked flight suit and helmet for a straw hat, shirt, and pants he could only button the bottom two buttons on. "A couple of the men gathered in my parachute and picked up my backpack, and then they said we had to leave quickly because the Japanese would be converging in ten minutes because they had an encampment nearby," Vraciu said.

Vraciu and his companions headed off in the direction of the nearby hills, passing through a small village along the way. After going by the village, the group entered a field of tall grass. They were led by a young Negrito boy who could see the path through the vegetation. "They picked me up a couple of times along the way and then put me down again," said Vraciu. After this happened to him the second time, the pilot asked what was going on. The guerrillas showed him that they had set bamboo traps in the tall grass to discourage the Japanese from following them. "One of these traps could rip off the whole calf of your leg, they said," Vraciu noted.

Because he did not know where he was being taken, Vraciu felt some concern about his would-be rescuers. His worries ended, however, when a couple of the young men in the group came over to him as they were heading into the hills and asked him two questions. "They wanted to know if movie star Madeleine Carroll was married the second time and whether Deanna Durbin [a Hollywood actress and singer] had any children yet," said Vraciu. "Now, I half smiled and thought to myself, 'Why am I worrying if this is all they were concerned about?'"

There remained, however, one nagging concern for the downed airman. Vraciu could not help but worry about how his new wife might take the news that he had not returned to the *Lexington*. Back in East Chicago, Kathryn Vraciu told a reporter from the *Chicago Tribune* that the last time she had heard from her husband had been in a December 10 letter in which he had written: "You won't be hearing from me again for a long time."

Fred Bakutis, commanding officer of Fighting Squadron 20, wrote a letter to Kathryn on December 18 in which he noted that although

Vraciu had been with the group only a short time, "his friendly, cheerful personality had already contributed much to the morale of the squadron. Moreover, he was a most competent pilot and a real asset to us. His missing status has been a great shock to all of us even though we hold considerable hope for his eventual recovery." After explaining the circumstances of how Vraciu was hit by Japanese anti-aircraft fire and offering some hope of his safe return, Bakutis cautioned Kathryn that it was not "beyond the realm of the possible, that he may, or already has fallen into enemy hands." Later, on Christmas Day, Kathryn received a dozen roses her husband had earlier ordered for her.

For several weeks Vraciu stayed in a guerrilla camp headed by Captain Alfred Bruce, a gaunt and thin survivor of the Bataan Death March who commanded the forces in the South Tarlac Military

An intelligence officer interviews pilots rescued by Philippine guerrillas. From left to right: Al Bruce, Allan Stover, and Francis Grassbaugh.

District. "I got there a couple of days too late for these guerrillas to take me over to the west coast of Luzon to be picked up by an American submarine," Vraciu noted, "but I was lucky because that submarine was sunk by a Japanese submarine." Vraciu and other American pilots rescued by the guerrillas stayed in a hut built over a chicken coop. Visitors to the camp could always tell how long the pilots had been in the Phillipines by the length of their beards, he recalled. On December 17 Bruce appointed Vraciu as a brevet major in the guerrilla forces and gave him the job as administration officer.

Food, a scarce item in the Philippines, became an important part of what the pilots thought about as they waited for American troops to invade Luzon. They soon became sick of constantly eating rice (upon his return to the United States, Vraciu banned rice from his family's dinner table for three years). For a change of pace, the Americans happily dined on what the Filipinos said was wild duck, but turned out to be fruit bats. "It wasn't too bad," Vraciu remembered. For their Christmas dinner, the pilots were lucky enough to have turkey. A rookie chef, Vraciu did not cook the turkey long enough, but the pilots were so hungry they ate the meat practically raw.

In addition to different food, Vraciu had to deal with the different customs and attitudes of the Filipino people, especially among the Negrito ethnic group (known for their small size). He was alarmed to discover that after an arranged marriage had been settled between two families, the parents of the prospective bride paid for the feast with captured Japanese money. Vraciu told the father of the bride that when the Americans liberated the Philippines, the enemy currency would no longer be good. The unconcerned father noted that they could always use the Japanese money for cigarette paper.

On another occasion, Vraciu witnessed a tribal council considering what to do about a member of the tribe whose wife ran off with a man from another village. There existed no precedents for divorce among the Negritos, so the council finally decided, Vraciu noted, that the abandoned husband's parents would get a rebate on the money they paid to the girl's family, and the husband received the errant bride's sister to take her place.

To help keep his mind occupied during his weeks with the guerrillas, Vraciu befriended a monkey he and the other pilots named Dugout Doug, an unflattering nickname that had been given to General Douglas MacArthur by American troops. Vraciu also kept notes on what was happening on Japanese airfields in the valley below. When his frustration level at not being in combat built high enough, he took a potshot with his .45-caliber pistol at a low flying enemy airplane. He learned, however, that his freedom came at a price. One day a visiting guerrilla told Vraciu that Japanese soldiers had killed twenty-two men from the village "near where I landed, trying to get them to tell them where I had been taken."

On the morning of January 9, 1945, approximately sixty-eight thousand troops from the U.S. Sixth Army landed on the coast of Lingayen Gulf and began the long march to retake Manila from the Japanese. News of the landing reached Bruce's guerrilla camp through another downed pilot who had been brought there. Bruce decided to send 150 members of his force north to hook up with the U.S. military. The guerrillas hoped to pass along to their allies information on the strength of Japanese troops in the area and to obtain arms and ammunition to continue their fight. The activity aroused Vraciu's interest, and he received permission from Bruce to join the small guerrilla group. Before leaving, Vraciu asked Bruce if there was anything he wanted, he would try, when he rejoined his squadron, to fly over his territory and drop it to him. Bruce thought about what he wanted for a moment and replied: "Two cans of beer."

Just prior to starting out, the guerrilla force's leader, Major Alberto Stockton, suffered a recurrence of malaria. "Just like that, I found myself in charge—a navy lieutenant," laughed Vraciu. "I was called major and had an aide I called Wednesday." For the next week, the group, armed only with a few pistols and rifles with no ammunition, evaded Japanese patrols and made its way toward the U.S. lines, growing larger and larger in size as they passed through various villages. "They [the Filipinos who joined] wanted to get in on the action with the Americans coming in," he noted. "Some called them 'sunshine patriots.'"

On its journey, the group stopped for lunch (rice) in the village of Mayuntoc. While there, Vraciu met the local mayor and an American woman married to a Filipino who lived in the village. While together the three of them read leaflets dropped by U.S. planes and signed by Sergio Osmeña, president of the Philippines. The leaflet called upon Filipinos to rally behind General MacArthur "so that the enemy may feel the full strength of our outraged people."

Suddenly, a member of another guerrilla group came face to face with Vraciu and half pointed a rifle at the pilot. "He could see that I wasn't a Filipino, and he appeared to be a little puzzled about what to do," said Vraciu. At first, the guerrilla mistook Vraciu for a member of the Hukbalahap, saying, "You Huk!" The pilot told him he was an American and, realizing what he was about to say sounded like a scene from a bad Hollywood film, told him: "Take me to your leader."

As the two men went down the trail, one of Vraciu's men ran

toward him for protection. Members of the other guerrilla group, under the control of an American survivor of the Bataan Death March named Albert Hendrickson from the North Tarlac area, fired and killed one member of Vraciu's band and seriously wounded another man. Visibly outraged, an angry Vraciu ordered the shooting to stop and yelled at the opposing force's commander that while the Americans were trying to wrest control of the Philippines from the Japanese, they were spending "more time killing each other than you were fighting the Japs!" The shooting ended, and the two groups combined forces and agreed to travel to Hendrickson's camp.

On the nighttime journey to Hendrickson's camp, Vraciu traveled in style, riding on the back of a small horse. Unfortunately, the horse was none too pleased at having a rider, and attempted to bite him whenever he could. About two hundred yards from the entrance to Hendrickson's camp, the horse finally got the better of the American pilot. "He just laid down and wouldn't go another yard," Vraciu recalled. "He made me walk the rest of the way."

Vraciu spent the next four days with Hendrickson's forces. In that time, he came to believe that Hendrickson had let his power go to his head. The former private had threatened the Filipinos in his area that if they did not provide him with food and alcohol he would have them labeled as pro-Jap (Japanese sympathizers) when American forces arrived. Hendrickson could tell that Vraciu did not approve of his leadership and asked him why he did not like him. "'No, it's not that,' Vraciu said. 'You're just enjoying this too much!' I said, 'You're going to have a hell of a time when you get back stateside.'"

After a few days of inactivity, Vraciu, anxious to connect with the advancing U.S. forces, told Hendrickson he would be taking his guerrilla group and leaving the next morning. Hendrickson seemed reluctant to have his group leave, telling Vraciu that if the American army planned on coming into his territory, they should report to him. When Vraciu indicated he planned on leaving no matter what, Hendrickson changed his mind and agreed to have his men go as well. That evening, the camp was on alert for a possible Japanese attack from across the river to the west. Someone gave Vraciu a carbine and he lay out that night with the others waiting for the enemy to strike. As he peered through the darkness, Vraciu remembered asking himself: "What is a good fighter pilot doing laying on his stomach in the middle of this God-forsaken country?"

Late the next morning, Vraciu participated in what he called the "strangest join-up of forces on the American side during the war." Both guerrilla groups marched together up the Philippine National Highway and were led by a bugler and three men displaying the flags of the United States, Philippines, and the guerrilla forces. "Following the flags came twelve of us 'chosen few' on horseback," said Vraciu. "This horse was a little bigger and didn't try to bite me."

As the group passed through villages on its way north, it picked up small groups of women, children, and dogs, who joined the march. This strange procession drew the attention of an American Avenger aircraft attempting to figure out who they were. "We'd just wave at the plane and wonder what kind of thoughts the crew may have had about us," Vraciu noted.

The group finally came upon an advance outpost manned by what Vraciu remembered as a six-foot, eight-inch-tall private who did not know what to do with what he saw. The soldier decided to let someone else deal with the problem, telling Vraciu: "Da sergeant's down da road." The group continued on and finally came to the outskirts of the 129th Infantry Regiment, a former National Guard unit from Illinois.

"When they found out I was from the Chicago area," said Vraciu, "there were warm feelings all around. They quickly broke out coffee, wafers, and beans." After visiting for a short time, the pilot mentioned that he had valuable information that he had to turn over to the commanding general. "They called somebody right away," said Vraciu, who while waiting said goodbye to his guerrillas.

In no time at all, a one-star general showed up with an aide, and Vraciu joined them for a trip to the city of Camiling in an American Jeep. The general drove and Vraciu sat beside him in the right seat. The two men talked on their way to General Robert S. Beighter's headquarters in Camiling. During a lull in conversation, the aide sitting

As fellow USS *Lexington* pilot Bud Duning looks on, Vraciu displays a captured Japanese lugar pistol he obtained during his time in the Philippines.

in the back seat said, "You're Vraciu, aren't you?" It turned out that
both men had attended DePauw University in Greencastle, Indiana,
at the same time and that the aide was in the class behind Vraciu. At
Camiling, Vraciu had lunch with Beightler and remembered devouring
an entire loaf of bread, which the general "got a big kick out of."

After catching up on his sleep and receiving a new set of clothes,
Vraciu received a ride to the harbor to report back to the navy. Going
up the gangplank of the USS *Wasatch*, a *Mount McKinley*-class
command ship, on January 19, Vraciu ran across a war correspondent
who had been on the *Lexington* during the Marianas Turkey Shoot. The
reporter, Elmont Waite, recognized the pilot despite the one-inch beard
he had grown and obtained a fast interview with him after he promised
to get word back to Vraciu's wife that he had been rescued.

In the interview, Waite called Vraciu as "indestructible" and noted
that the pilot boarded the ship carrying a Japanese saber and Luger
pistol as souvenirs of his stay in the Philippines. Kathryn received news
of her husband's return at her family's home on East 142nd Street
in East Chicago. "It's wonderful," Kathryn said, adding that she and
Vraciu's mother and father had never given up hope that he would
return alive and well. "I had a feeling I might hear something about
him soon."

Vraciu found himself on a succession of ships and planes as he
made his way back to the *Lexington*. He finally arrived at Ulithi where
the carrier was anchored and rejoined his squadron, still wearing the
beard he had grown while in the Philippines. "The executive officer of
the ship worked hard to make me shave my beard," Vraciu recalled.
"He was being very tactful, and he gave me a razor. He didn't want
me to have a beard on board the ship. That wasn't kosher back then."
Unfortunately for Vraciu, near the end of January Fighting Squadron

A clean shaven and rested Vraciu points to a map of Luzon in the Philippines to indicate where he had been shot down by the Japanese.

20 had received orders to return home; he would have to wait to try his luck again in the air against the Japanese.

Upon his return to Pearl Harbor, Vraciu hoped to be part of planned American carrier raids against Toyko. His hopes were dashed when officials informed him that he could not operate over enemy territory until the Philippines had been secured from the Japanese (if the enemy shot him down again, the navy did not want Vraciu to face the possibility of giving information on the guerrilla groups). While on leave, Vraciu had the opportunity to visit the Grumman Aircraft Corporation operation at Long Island, New York. While there, he flew Grumman's newest fighter, the F8F Bearcat, the plane designed to replace the Hellcat.

Vraciu became even more familiar with the Bearcat when the navy assigned him as a test pilot (Tactical Test) at the Naval Air Test Center at Patuxent River, Maryland, for the last few months of the war. "I did the evaluation of the Bearcat, since I'd flown it at the factory," he said, adding that it would have been a great plane to pilot in combat.

As American forces made their way closer and closer to the home islands of the Japanese Empire, enemy troops attempted to halt the drive by giving their lives in greater and greater numbers. Landings on the islands of Iwo Jima and Okinawa were bloody affairs, with thousands of casualties on both sides (more than a hundred and twenty thousand Americans and Japanese were killed during the fighting on Okinawa alone).

U.S. officials were expecting the number of dead and wounded to increase to staggering proportions when allied soldiers invaded Japan and the other countries it still occupied. One Allied soldier later said of the battles to come that he did not expect he and his friends to survive.

"We would have been murdered in the biggest massacre of the war," he said. "They [the Japanese] would have annihilated the lot of us." But by using a new weapon—an atomic bomb—the United States hoped to finally end the bloodshed in the Pacific.

1

PEACE

What Yoshihiro Kimura, a third-grade student in Hiroshima, Japan, remembers about the morning of August 6, 1945, is how normal the day started for his family. While his older brother cooked some fish to take with him to his job, Kimura and his sister got ready for school. At his classroom, Kimura talked with his friends about the war his country was fighting against the United States and hurried home when he heard an air-raid warning. He returned to school when the all-clear sounded.

While the students at Kimura's school talked, waiting for their teacher to return, they heard the sound of an airplane—an American B-29 Superfortress bomber. "All of a sudden, something white like a parachute fell out from the plane," Kimura recalled. "Five or six seconds later, everything turned yellow. It was like I'd looked right at the sun. Then there was a big sound a second or two later and everything went dark. Stones and tiles fell on my head and I was knocked out for a bit." Kimura managed to crawl from the wreckage of his school and saw bodies scattered about, many of them with burned-black faces. He looked down and saw that the skin of his right arm from the elbow to his fingers had peeled off.

Kimura and thousands of others in Hiroshima had become the first victims of a new type of weapon in war—the atomic bomb. Developed by scientists working as part of a two-billion-dollar effort by the American government at a top-secret facility in Los Alamos,

New Mexico, the bomb harnessed tremendous power, with a force equal to twenty thousand tons of the explosive TNT. When it had first been tested at the army air force's Alamogordo Bombing Range, located about two hundred miles south of Los Alamos, J. Robert Oppenheimer, the project's research director, had been stunned by the bomb's enormous power. A thought flashed through his mind of a line from a Hindu epic called the Bhagavad-Gita: "I am become Death, the shatterer of worlds."

The Hiroshima bomb had been dropped on its target by a B-29 bomber called the *Enola Gay* and piloted by Colonel Paul Tibbets Jr. from the 509th Composite Group flying from North Field on the island of Tinian in the Pacific. Nicknamed "Little Boy," the weapon dropped on Hiroshima exploded about seventeen hundred feet above the city's Shima Surgical Hospital. The explosion devastated the city, destroying approximately sixty thousand buildings and killing approximately eighty thousand people almost in an instant (thousands more died later due to their injuries or radiation sickness).

After dropping the bomb, Tibbets called on his radio to ask Bob Caron, the tail gunner on the *Enola Gay*, if he could count the number of fires burning in Hiroshima. "I said, 'Count them? Hell I gave up when there were

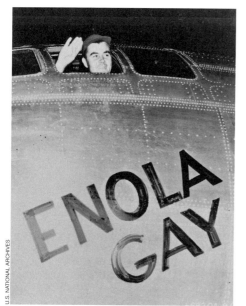

Colonel Paul W. Tibbets Jr., pilot of the plane that dropped the atomic bomb on Hiroshima, waves from his cockpit before takeoff on August 6, 1945.

With reporters crowded around his desk at the White House, President Harry Truman announces the Japanese surrender, August 14, 1945.

about fifteen, they were coming too fast to count," Caron said. As he snapped photographs of the distinctive mushroom cloud caused by the blast, Caron compared looking at the sight to "a peep into hell."

In Washington, D.C., President Harry S. Truman, who had assumed office following the April 12 death of Franklin D. Roosevelt, warned Japan's government that America was prepared to destroy "every productive enterprise the Japanese have above ground in any city. We shall destroy their docks, their factories, and their communications. Let there be no mistake; we shall completely destroy Japan's power to make war."

Truman made good on his threat. Hearing no response to a call by the Allied powers for Japan's unconditional surrender, a second atomic bomb, nicknamed "Fat Man," was dropped by a B-29 from Tinian on its target, the industrial city of Nagasaki. More than forty thousand people were killed and another sixty thousand were injured. By that time, Japan also had to deal with another enemy, as the Soviet Union had declared war and thousands of Russian troops were attacking Japanese forces in Manchuria.

Although some in the Japanese military wanted to fight to the death, the combined shocks of the atomic bombs and the Russian invasion prompted the government officials in Japan to notify the Allies on August 14 that it intended to surrender. "The time has come," said Emperor Hirohito, "when we must bear the unbearable." On August 15 Japanese heard over the radio a recording of the emperor's speech announcing the nation's unconditional surrender. The broadcast marked the first time in the lives of most Japanese people to hear the voice of their emperor. Formal surrender documents were signed on September 2 onboard the battleship USS *Missouri* in Tokyo Bay. After the loss of fifty-five million lives, both military and civilian, around the globe, World War II was over.

When the war in Europe against Nazi Germany ended in early May 1945, approximately thirty divisions of troops were set to be transferred to the Pacific theater for the planned invasion of Japan, code-named Operation Downfall. More than seven hundred thousand troops already in the Pacific were scheduled to hit the island of Kyushu on November 1. Allied officers had no illusions about the cost to their men. General Douglas MacArthur told Secretary of War Henry Stimson that the invasion of Japan would result in "over a million casualties [dead and wounded] to American forces alone." In anticipation of the large number of losses, the U.S. government

Above: The devastation caused by the atomic bomb dropped on the Japanese port city of Nagasaki. In the background are the remains of a Roman Catholic cathedral.
Right: A dense column of smoke rises more than sixty thousand feet into the air over Nagasaki, August 8, 1945.

manufactured a half million Purple Hearts to honor those wounded in battle.

The news of peace spread like wildfire to the fighting men preparing for the invasion. Paul Fussell, who had fought the Germans as a lieutenant with the Forty-fifth Infantry Division, noted that although he had been wounded seriously enough to be judged 40 percent disabled after the war, he had been one of the thousands of GIs selected to hit the Japanese home islands. When he and other members of his outfit learned that because of the atomic bombs they would not have to "rush up the beaches near Tokyo assault-firing while being machine-gunned, mortared, and shelled, for all the practiced phlegm of our tough façades we broke down and cried with relief and joy. We were going to live. We were going to grow to adulthood after all."

Back in the United States, Alex Vraciu was stationed at the Naval Air Test Center at Patuxent River, Maryland, testing and evaluating new aircraft to help win final victory in the Pacific. "Pure and simple," he said, "Hiroshima and Nagasaki came as a totally welcome surprise, for we all had expected a long war and invasion of Japan." Although historians have debated for years on whether or not Japan might have surrendered even if the atomic bombs had not been used, Vraciu and his comrades at the time believed that "thousands and thousands of American lives were saved" because of Truman's decision to use the new weapon.

With the war over, the thoughts of the sailors, pilots, soldiers, and marines turned to home and their life in peacetime. Many left the service and took advantage of the GI Bill, legislation passed by Congress in 1944 that offered veterans aid in obtaining education at colleges and universities as well as loans for buying homes. Vraciu, who had ended the war as the fourth highest scoring navy fighter pilot,

Above: Jubilant residents of Indianapolis display copies of the *Indianapolis News* announcing the Japanese surrender, ending the fighting in World War II. **Inset:** General Douglas MacArthur signs the official surrender documents during ceremonies on the battleship USS *Missouri* in Tokyo Bay on September 2, 1945. Standing behind MacArthur are American lieutenant general Jonathan Wainwright and British lieutenant general A. E. Percival.

had made plans to leave the service. Those plans changed, however, when he received an invitation for lunch at the Navy Department in Washington, D.C., from Captain R. L. Johnson, the former commanding officer of the aircraft carrier USS *Independence.*

During the lunch, Johnson asked Vraciu to help him start the Naval and Marine Air Reserve program (civilians and part-time military personnel who would be ready to fight if the country had another war). Johnson had been given the assignment by Admiral Marc Mitscher. Vraciu told Johnson the job looked fantastic, but that he had already given his six-month notification asking to be released from navy duty. The captain then said, "I'll take that chance if you will," Vraciu remembered. He noted that a "fighter pilot is supposed to make up his mind in a hurry," and he did, accepting Johnson's offer. With the assumption of this job came the spot promotion in rank to lieutenant commander.

For the next six years, Vraciu "fought the battle of the budget" at the Navy Department, and later the Pentagon, where he was responsible for determining all the personnel and aircraft complements, and the numbering of squadrons for the twenty-eight bases across the country. "It was the best job I ever had in my life," he said.

Although he felt good about his job in Washington, Vraciu still dreamed of a position every fighter pilot ultimately desired—command of his own fighter squadron. After postwar staff duty in the Navy Department, serving as jet training officer at Los Alamitos Naval Air Station in California, and Naval Post-Graduate School at Monterey, Vraciu served as communications officer onboard the carrier USS *Hornet.* With the help of twelve bright young officers, Vraciu and his team on the *Hornet* received the "E" for Excellence Award for the entire Pacific Fleet. "I figured for an aviator to get that, that's good," he noted.

In the postwar years, Vraciu remained in the navy, working at the Pentagon, serving on the USS *Hornet*, and commanding his own fighter squadron. His children particularly enjoyed the squadron picnics with unlimited soft drinks and hot dogs.

While the *Hornet* underwent an angle deck and steam catapult conversion in its flight deck at the naval shipyard at Bremerton, Washington, Vraciu received a call from a friend on the staff at ComAir Pac in San Diego asking if he would like to take over command of Fighting Squadron 51. "How about this afternoon?" Vraciu replied. He led the squadron for the next twenty-two months. "I never worked so hard in my life," he said of those days. Vraciu's hard work paid off. In January 1957 his squadron won the Pacific Fleet air-to-air gunnery competition flying North American FJ-3 Fury jet fighters (a swept-wing navy aircraft based on the U.S. Air Force's famous F-86 Sabre jet that had achieved numerous victories during the Korean War) to represent the Pacific Fleet.

Like other World War II-era pilots, Vraciu had to transition from flying propeller-powered aircraft to jet fighters, including the FJ-3 Fury pictured below. The swept-wing plane featured folding wings and a longer nose strut to absorb the shock of landing on a carrier.

COURTESY ALEX VRACIU

Vraciu formally takes over as commander of Fighting Squadron 51. He served in that job from 1956 to 1958, when he became commanding officer of an advanced jet training unit at the Kingsville Naval Air Station in Texas.

Just a few months later, in April 1957, Vraciu and his squadron
competed in the navy's annual five-day Air Weapons Meet in El Centro,
California, that involved navy and marine pilots from both the Pacific
and Atlantic fleets—an early version of the "Top Gun" competition
made famous by the 1986 Tom Cruise movie of the same name.
Fighting Squadron 51 defeated every other navy squadron, being edged
out only by a marine squadron based in El Toro, California.

Although he had not fired a gun in twelve years, Vraciu said he
practiced and thought if he finished in the top ten in the individual
competition, he would "be pleased as punch, especially with that

Vraciu (at center) stands with officials and other members of Fighting Squadron
51 following the Air Weapons Meet in which he won top honors. Vraciu said he
"did everything I humanly could think of" to prepare for the contest, including
extra gunnery practice in the FJ-3 Fury.

long delay." The previous year's winner, a pilot from the Atlantic fleet, had set a new record. "I thought he needed a little competition," said Vraciu, who broke the record.

When the scores were counted, Vraciu won the trophy for High Individual Air-to-Air Competition. Admiral Felix Stump, commander-in-chief of the Pacific Fleet, sent the former ace a congratulatory telegram that read: "I'm delighted to hear that you are 'Top Gun' in jets in peace as you were in Hellcats in war." Achieving the top honor in the 1957 competition later turned into "more respect" from Vraciu's grandchildren after they saw the *Top Gun* film.

After twenty-two years in the navy, Vraciu, who had reached the rank of commander, retired from the service on December 31, 1963. Awaiting retirement, he finished his military career as the public information officer at the Alameda Naval Air Station near Oakland, California. After his retirement from the navy, Vraciu and his wife Kathryn remained in California, moving to Los Altos in 1971 and Danville in 1975, where Vraciu worked as a trust officer for Wells Fargo Bank. The couple had five children—Carol, Robert, Linda, Marilyn, and Marc—and had fourteen major moves during Vraciu's time in naval service.

Today, Vraciu is retired and living in Danville. His wife, Kathryn, died in 2003 after an eight-year battle with Alzheimer's disease. Over the years, Vraciu's dedicated service during the war has led some to argue that he deserved far more recognition than the decorations he received for his aerial exploits—a Navy Cross, a Distinguished Flying Cross with two gold stars, and an Air Medal with three gold stars. After his spectacular victories in the First Battle of the Philippine Sea, Vraciu had been recommended by all seven of the on-the-scene admirals to receive the country's highest honor—the Medal of Honor. An admiral

Above: The Vraciu family. From top right to bottom: Alex, Kathryn, Carol, Robert, Linda, Marilyn, and Marc. **Right:** Alex and Kathryn enjoy a dance together in 1980 during the couple's retirement in Danville, California.

in Hawaii, however, improperly processed the recommendation and downgraded the award to a Navy Cross, in effect, ignoring three of the four events listed in the citation.

In 1991 and 1993 Indiana congressman Andrew Jacobs Jr. introduced joint resolutions in the House of Representatives calling upon the president to award the Medal of Honor to Vraciu for "his superlatively heroic service to our Nation." Although Vraciu believes he never received a fair and open hearing from the navy, he did note: "You don't fight a war for medals." Others, however, continue to fight on Vraciu's behalf, even establishing a Web site (http://www.alexvraciu.net/) calling on Americans to support efforts to get the federal government to award Vraciu the Medal of Honor.

Vraciu has become a popular speaker on his World War II career in front of schoolchildren and civic and business groups. During a talk at a Kiwanis Club meeting in California, an audience member asked him a serious question—what had it felt like to shoot someone down in wartime? After pondering the question, Vraciu noted that he had no doubts that if he was in the same position and had to do it tomorrow, he "would have no qualms about it," as he continues to remember Pearl Harbor and the friends that he lost along the way.

LEARN MORE ABOUT ALEX VRACIU AND WORLD WAR II IN THE PACIFIC

Interviews

Author with Alex Vraciu, August 13 and 14, 2008, Danville, CA.

Douglas E. Clanin with Alex Vraciu, June 14 and 15, 1990, Danville, CA. Interview available from the William Henry Smith Memorial Library, Indiana Historical Society, Indianapolis, IN.

Ronald E. Marcello with Alex Vraciu, October 9, 1994, Kerrville, Texas. Interview available from the University of North Texas Oral History Collection, Denton, TX.

Books

Stephen E. Ambrose, *American Heritage New History of World War II* (New York: Viking, 1997).

———, *The Good Fight: How World War II Was Won* (New York: Atheneum Books for Young Readers, 2001).

Gerald Astor, *Wings of Gold: The U.S. Naval Campaign in World War II* (New York: Presidio Press, 2004).

Eric Bergerud, *Touched with Fire: The Land War in the South Pacific* (New York: Viking, 1996).

Tom Brokaw, *The Greatest Generation* (New York: Random House, 1998).

Victor Brooks, *Hell is upon Us: D-Day in the Pacific, June–August 1944* (Cambridge, MA: Da Capo Press, 2005).

Thomas B. Buell, *The Quiet Warrior: A Biography of Admiral Raymond A. Spruance* (Boston: Little, Brown and Company, 1974).

Elin B. Christianson, *Lake County Communities, Past and Present* (Hobart, IN: Hobart Historical Society, 2001).

Beverly Roberts Dawson, *Glenview Naval Air Station* (Charleston, SC: Arcadia Publishing, 2007).

Steve Ewing and John B. Lundstrom, *Fateful Rendezvous: The Life of Butch O'Hare* (Annapolis, MD: Naval Institute Press, 1997).

Paul Fussell, *Thank God for the Atom Bomb and Other Essays* (New York: Summit Books, 1988).

———, *Wartime: Understanding and Behavior in the Second World War* (New York: Oxford University Press, 1989).

Thomas M. Goldstein, Katherine V. Dillon, and J. Michael Wenger, *Rain of Ruin: A Photographic History of Hiroshima and Nagasaki* (Washington, DC: Brassey's, 1995).

Max Hastings, *Retribution: The Battle for Japan, 1944–45* (New York: Alfred A. Knopf, 2008).

Chester G. Hearn, *Carriers in Combat: The Air War at Sea*

(Mechanicsburg, PA: Stackpole Books, 2005).

Mark Henry, *The U.S. Navy in World War II*
(Oxford, England: Osprey Publishing, 2002).

Edward Jablonski, *Airwar*, vol. 3; *Outraged Skies*
(Garden City, NY: Doubleday and Company, 1971).

Philip Kaplan, *Fly Navy: Naval Aviators and Carrier Aviation—A History*
(London, UK: MetroBooks, 2001).

Robert Leckie, *Strong Men Armed: The United States Marines against Japan*
(New York: Random House, 1962).

Gerald F. Linderman, *The World Within War: America's Combat Experience
in World War II* (New York: Free Press, 1997).

Ernest A. McKay, *Carrier Strike Force: Pacific Air Combat in World War II*
(New York: Julian Messner, 1981).

John C. McManus, *Deadly Sky: The American Combat Airman in World War II* (Novato, CA:
Presidio Press, 2000).

William Manchester, *American Caesar: Douglas McArthur, 1880–1964*
(Boston: Little, Brown and Company, 1978).

Powell A. Moore, *The Calumet Region: Indiana's Last Frontier*
(Indianapolis: Indiana Historical Bureau, 1959).

Samuel Eliot Morison, *History of United States Naval Operations in World War II*,
vol. 7, *Aleutians, Gilberts, and Marshalls, June 1942–April 1944*
(1951; reprint, Edison, NJ: Castle Books, 2001).

———, *History of United States Naval Operations in World War II*, vol. 8.
New Guinea and the Marianas, March 1944–August 1944 (1953; reprint, Urbana
and Chicago: University of Illinois Press, 2002).

Arata Osada, ed, *Children of Hiroshima* (Tokyo: Publishing Committee for Children of
Hiroshima, 1980).

Michael Paterson, *Battle for the Skies* (Cincinnati, OH: David and Charles, 2004).

Clifton J. Phillips, *Indiana in Transition: The Emergence of an Industrial Commonwealth,
1880–1920* (Indianapolis: Indiana Historical Bureau and Indiana Historical Society, 1968).

Dominick A. Pisano, *To Fill the Skies with Pilots: The Civilian Pilot Training Program, 1939–
46* (Urbana and Chicago: University of Illinois Press, 1993).

E. B. Potter and Chester W. Nimitz, eds, *Triumph in the Pacific: The Navy's Struggle against
Japan* (Englewood Cliffs, NJ: Prentice-Hall, 1963).

Otto C. Romanelli, *Blue Ghost Memoirs: USS* Lexington*, CV-16, 1943–1945* (Paducah, KY:
Turner Publishing, 2002).

Edward H. Sims, *Greatest Fighter Missions of the Top Navy and Marine Aces of World War II*
(New York: Ballantine Books, 1962).

E. B. Sledge, *With the Old Breed at Peleiu and Okinawa* (1981; reprint, New York: University
of Oxford Press, 1990).

David Smurthwaite, *The Pacific War Atlas: 1941–1945* (New York: Facts on File, 1995).

Paul M. Somers, *Lake Michigan's Aircraft Carriers* (Charleston, SC: Arcadia Publishing, 2003).

Ronald H. Spector, *Eagle against the Sun: The American War with Japan* (New York: Free Press, 1985).

Rafael Steinberg, *Island Fighting* (Chicago: Time-Life Books, 1978).

Mark Stille, *U.S. Navy Aircraft Carriers 1942–45: WWII-Built Ships* (Oxford, UK: Osprey Publishing, 2007).

Theodore Taylor, *The Magnificent Mitscher* (1954; reprint, Annapolis, MD: Naval Institute Press, 2006).

Studs Terkel, *"The Good War": An Oral History of World War II* (New York: Ballantine, 1984).

Barrett Tillman, *Clash of the Carriers: The True Story of the Marianas Turkey Shoot of World War II* (New York: NAL Caliber, 2005).

———, *Hellcat Aces of World War 2* (Oxford, UK: Osprey Publishing, 1996).

———, *Hellcat: The F6F in World War II* (Annapolis, MD: Naval Institute Press, 1979).

William Tuohy, *America's Fighting Admirals: Winning the War at Sea in World War II* (Saint Paul, MN: Zenith Press, 2007).

Stephen Walker, *Shockwave: Countdown to Hiroshima* (New York: HarperCollins, 2005).

Thomas W. Zeiler, *Unconditional Defeat: Japan, American, and the End of World War II* (Wilmington, DE: Scholarly Resources, 2004).

Articles and other Media

"Families in the Calumet Region during the Depression of the 1930s," *Steel Shavings* 13 (1977).

Richard M. Hill, "Hellcat 40467: The History of One F6F." *American Aviation Historical Society Journal* (Fall 1972).

Merle Miller, "What's Butch O'Hare Doing These Days?" *Yank: The Army Weekly*, August 22, 1943.

Dave Parsons, "Fighter Tactics in World War II," *Naval Aviation News* (July–August 1993).

Matt Portz, "Aviation Training and Expansion (Part 1)," *Naval Aviation News*, (July–August 1990).

Walter Simmons, "'Splash Six Japs,'" *Chicago Tribune*, September 17, 1944.

"The Zero Killers," *Dogfights: The Complete Season 1*, History Channel DVD, 2006.

Barrett Tillman. "Hellcats over Truk," *U.S. Naval Institute Proceedings* (March 1977).

John F. Wukovits. "Greatest Aircraft Carrier Duel," *World War II* (July 1994).

World War II Web Sites

"A People at War" National Archives and Records Administration, http://www.archives.gov/exhibits/a_people_at_war/a_people_at_war.html.

Alex Vraciu, Hellcat Ace, http://www.alexvraciu.net/#Vraciu.

Dictionary of American Naval Fighting Ships Online,
    http://www.hazegray.org/danfs/.

Hiroshima Peace Memorial Museum,
    http://www.hiroshima-spirit.jp/en/museum/index.html.

The Manhattan Project, Office of History and Heritage Resources,
    U.S. Department of Energy,
    http://www.cfo.doe.gov/me70/manhattan/index.htm.

The National Museum of the Pacific War,
    http://www.nimitz-museum.org/.

National Naval Aviation Museum,
    http://www.navalaviationmuseum.org/.

National World War II Memorial,
    http://www.wwiimemorial.com/.

Naval Historical Center,
    http://www.history.navy.mil/.

USS *Arizona* Memorial,
    http://www.nps.gov/usar/.

USS *Independence,*
    http://www.cvl-22.com/pics3.html.

USS *Intrepid* Sea, Air, and Space Museum,
    http://www.intrepidmuseum.org/.

USS *Lexington* Museum on the Bay,
    http://www.usslexington.com/.

World War II,
    http://www.history.com/minisites/worldwartwo.

World War II Documents, The Avalon Project, Yale Law School,
    http://avalon.law.yale.edu/subject_menus/wwii.asp.

INDEX